HEADS! & Tales

Uncle Bill's Musings on the Theatrical Experience

To Ed
all the Best

HEADS! & Tales

Uncle Bill's Musings on the Theatrical Experience

Bill Sapsis

Sapsis Publications
Lansdowne, PA

HEADS! and Tales
Bill Sapsis

Sapsis Publications
233 N. Lansdowne Ave.
Lansdowne, PA 19050
800.727.7471
215.228.0888
www.sapsis-rigging.com

Edited by Lynn Kennedy

Based on articles by Bill Sapsis published in the Sapsis Rigging newsletter HEADS! © 1993 - 2007, edited by Sarah Gowan.

Original illustrations ©2007 Kim Feigenbaum
Cover photo ©2007 by Christopher Harris
Cover design, interior design & production by Sarah Gowan

ISBN: 978-0-9797039-0-4

Printed and bound in the United States of America

For Emma, Garrett and Jordan

Contents

Acknowledgments

Look. It's a book! What do you know, I've written a book. Yes, I'm as surprised as you are. But if you think I did this all by my lonesome you'd be very, very wrong. Lots of people had a hand in this one way or another. And I'd like to take a moment and thank them.

As you may know, this book started out as a series of articles I wrote for the Sapsis Rigging, Inc. newsletter, HEADS!, *that started out in print form in 1993. (You remember snail mail?) Rhonda Wenner did a remarkable job as the graphic artist. It was, after all, before the days of Adobe Photoshop. She did it all by hand. Rhonda also served as a proofreader/editor, a job she shared with Sarah Gowan. These two talented people helped lay the foundation for the newsletter and I owe them both a great big thank you.*

When we shifted over to an electronic version, Sarah took over the graphic arts duties and the proofreading. There is no one on this planet who has read these articles more than she has. She has saved me from embarrassing myself more than I care to admit. I am eternally in her debt.

David Roger has been wonderfully free with his advice and encouragement. Tom Young took time out of an insanely busy schedule to review early versions of the book and, with David, help keep me on course.

Greg Williams not only provided the moral support that kept me from running screaming from the room on occasion but also introduced me to Kim Feigenbaum. Kim provided the illustrations you see gracing these pages.

Eddie Raymond has been a friend and a source of encouragement since we met during the early days of the ETCP Rigging Certification Program. Not only has he reviewed a number of drafts of this book, but he also wrote the forward. He has helped me make a fool of myself at ESTA functions and on the ski slopes. Rocky Paulson, who shared chairmanship duties with Eddie and me at the ETCP, may not know it, but he's been an inspiration to me since we met back in the early '90s.

His rigging abilities are legendary, but it was his teaching skills and his joie d' vivre that, for me, made him an icon of the industry.

Jay Glerum and I haven't always seen eye to eye (I think I come up to his tie tack) but his book and his dedication to safety in the industry have always been an inspiration for me.

And then there's Randy Davidson. How could I ever forget Dr. Doom? He laid the groundwork for all that was to come after and I, along with many thousand of other folks, am in his debt.

Donna Frankel has been my friend and confidant for a long time and her moral support has helped me get through the dark periods that invariably creep into the writing process.

Lynn Kennedy has been editor, friend, supporter and taskmaster all rolled into one. We worked together when she was with ESTA's journal, Protocol, *and I was thrilled when she agreed to edit this book. Without her questions, prods and pushes, I doubt it would ever have seen the light of day.*

And finally, I want to thank all of you who not only read my articles over the years, but also offered your comments and encouragement. I don't have the words to tell you how much your notes, email and phone calls meant to me. Harry Donovan once called to tell me how much he liked a fall arrest article. People asked to reprint articles for their classrooms and IA offices. I even found one taped (yes, with gaffers' tape) to the bulletin board of the Sun City Arena in South Africa.

And so to all of you, named and unnamed, I offer my deepest and sincerest thanks. Without you this book wouldn't have happened and I'd be tending bar in some shot and beer joint down by the river.

Foreword

There are quite a few books on the market about theatre rigging and safety. Most of them have information that is relevant to those working in the industry, but if you're like me, about half way through these tomes your eyes start to glaze over and you find yourself daydreaming about things more interesting and entertaining than fleet angles and load distribution.

You see, the key to communicating almost anything is this; not only does the author need to have something relevant to say, but that person needs to say it in a way that captures your attention as a reader. If it isn't relevant, you have no reason to spend the time to read it; if it doesn't keep your interest, you're not likely to retain much of the information.

The book you have in your hands at this moment has both elements. It is full of things that theatre technicians need to know to do their jobs and to do them safely, and it is presented in a way that is not only easy to read, but downright fun. Who would have thought that any discussion of technology and safety matters could be entertaining?

Well, Bill Sapsis did. He's been discussing the things that we do and how we do them for years. He's trained theatre technicians around the world. He's written articles for numerous publications about "the life" and about how we do our work. He's inspected our facilities and steered us in the right direction for our own good. In doing so he's seen the best and the worst of what can happen when we do our jobs.

Bill's numerous contributions to *HEADS!*, to the Stagecraft Digest web log and to most of the theatrical publications in this country are legends among stagehands. Over the years we've not only been blessed by his sage advice, but we've been entertained by his wry wit and served by his willingness to blaspheme the sacred halls of theatre by challenging tradition and custom and practice. He's made us ask ourselves, "Just 'cause we've always done it that way, does that make it right?" We've also shared the travails of fatherhood and life in general as we followed his personal travels and family experiences as they unfolded.

I had the good fortune to be introduced to Bill through the Rigging Skills Working Group in 2002. This was the group of volunteers put together by the Entertainment Services and Technology Association to lay the groundwork for a certification program aimed at verifying the skills of entertainment riggers. (What a concept!) Eventually Bill, Rocky Paulson of Stage Rigging and I chaired this group. The first Entertainment Technician Certification Program test was successfully launched at LDI in 2005.

In the years since we met I have been the grateful recipient of several reality checks, always mixed with a healthy dose of humor. I have repeatedly been impressed by Bill's willingness to share his expertise and by his dedication to the industry. I've been even more impressed by his ability to keep stagehands (myself included) laughing while imparting his advice; probably the best formula for teaching anyone, particularly for teaching old dogs new tricks.

I know that you will be both entertained and instructed as you read this book. There is no better way to learn something than while you are smiling throughout the lesson. So sit back, put your feet up and let the good times roll. Remember the lessons and pass them on. Remember to pass on the smiles as well.

Eddie Raymond
Vice President I.A.T.S.E. Local 16
San Francisco, California

Introduction

Back in the '70s, when I first started out in this business, safety wasn't much of an issue. In fact it was pretty much looked down on by everyone. Being a high steel rigger meant you were a macho kind of guy. If you showed up at a call with a harness you got laughed at. Everyone took risks. There was one guy I knew who used his rope to haul hoists in the air and then, at the end of the day, he'd rappel down out of the steel. On the same rope! Yup, the very same rope that he'd thrown over beams, that had been run over by a forklift or three and that had more knots tied in it than a macramé hammock.

Ultimately, people started getting hurt. There were some fatalities. And so safety awareness began creeping into the workplace. Riggers started wearing harnesses. Unfortunately they were climbing harnesses, because that's what we used when we went rock climbing. We thought that they'd be good for work also. We now know that we were wrong.

It was around this time that I was hit by a counterweight that had fallen from the loading bridge of a theatre in Orlando, Florida. Three months later a very good friend took a fall backstage in a New York City theatre and was killed. Those two incidents convinced me that safety should become a major focus of my career.

I started writing articles in the late '80s and early '90s. For the most part they were safety articles – how to keep from getting hurt while on the job and how to choose and use the proper equipment. These "Memos from Uncle Bill" seemed to go over well, so I kept writing. Safety topics tend to be a bit dry so I expanded my horizons and added articles on my travels and experiences in the business. After about ten years I had a pretty decent stash of material sitting around gathering dust.

Events of the past three or four years convinced me that somehow the safety message wasn't getting through to everyone who needed it. I was extremely frustrated by the number of accidents I was hearing about. So I did what I could to help address the situation. I wrote a book.

This book is actually a collection of my articles, though not in their original format. They've been updated and re-organized in an attempt to present them in an informative, yet still humorous, manner. I take safety issues very seriously but that doesn't mean I have to be serious all the time when I write about them.

The articles have been assembled so that there is a progression of sorts. As far as I'm concerned, good communications are key to everything we do in the rigging business and the lack of communication is the primary reason accidents happen. With that in mind I've started off with a discussion of what it takes to understand what's happening backstage and overhead before, during and after a show. There are too many people, myself included, who have paid the price for bad communications and have the scars to prove it.

The early chapters of the book are primarily devoted to discussions of a variety of rigging equipment and procedures we use to do our jobs well. I really enjoy working with rope and it was fun writing about it. I've given you tips on how to use and maintain your equipment as well as spot potential problems. There's also advice about things you should not do, stemming from years of learning the hard way.

Amateur riggers flying performers is one of my pet peeves. I don't know why people think flying a human around a stage is so easy and not dangerous. Ask Sandy Duncan how dangerous it can be. The article I included on this subject was well received when I first wrote it, not only here but also in several European countries.

Fall arrest is another subject close to my heart and that's reflected in the book. The original article was a response to several accidents that killed a couple of stagehands. I've expanded on that article and also pointed readers to additional sources of information on this critical topic. I'm hoping that we can dramatically reduce the number of fatalities in this business.

In some of the later chapters I've tried to convey a sense of what it's been like to be in this business for thirty-plus years. I've been very fortunate in that my work has taken me all over the world. Believe it or not, there was a time when you didn't find a

McDonald's in places like Taipei or Paris. There really were places with local food. You could find the local culture around the next bend in the road. I didn't want to lose that. I hope you'll enjoy sharing my travels, tales and reflections.

I've never really considered myself a writer or an educator, just a rigger that likes to write. My goal in publishing this book is to help keep you safe on the job. We work in a wonderful business and I'm honored to be a part of it. If this book helps you better understand what you are doing at work, gives you some pointers on how to do your job better and occasionally puts a smile on your face, then I'll feel like I've done my job.

Enjoy.

-1-
Be Safe

Back in 1985 I ran the rigging installation at the Palladium, one of the first mega clubs in New York City. Over a four-month period we installed about 25,000 pounds of gear, all of it suspended over the dance floor. At the same time the rest of the building was being transformed from a theatre (it was originally the Academy of Music) to a hipper club look. One thing I found a little curious was that during the entire construction period no one approached me for my credentials. Not to say there weren't building inspectors crawling all over the place. There were. They checked the exit lights. They checked the aisle lights. They inspected the plumbing. They even had a guy inspecting the soda guns at the bar. But did anyone come up to me at any time to see if I knew what I was doing? Nope. Here I was with all this stuff that was going to hang fifty feet above the glitterati and there was no one checking up on me. (But hey, ya gotta make sure the urinals are at the proper height, right?)

Now fast-forward about twenty years. Bette Midler had a monster show on the road. I got calls from various venue managers asking if I could come over and check out their rigging steel. They were worried about how much weight her rig was going to put on their roof structures. Now, don't get me wrong, I think it's great that they were calling me, but no one, and I really do mean no one, called with more than two days lead time. What was I supposed to do in two days?

And then there's the case of the grid in the Atlantic City Convention Center. During the load-in of a pop music show the grid collapsed. I'm not sure we'll ever know what the root cause of that failure was, but it's a safe bet that they overloaded the structure. Trusses don't usually fail when there is too little weight on them, eh?

So I'm wondering. Maybe things haven't changed all that much in the last twenty years. It looks to me like we're still having issues with getting accurate information to the right people. I know that safety (and its twin brother, liability) is all the rage these days, but are we really doing all we can to make sure accidents don't happen? I'm thinking maybe not.

I marvel sometimes at just how lucky we've been. I mean, here we are running around the country, and the world for that matter, and it feels like half the time only half of us have a clue as to what's going on. Road guys constantly complain to me about the venues they play. According to them there's always something wrong. Maybe the roof is too low or the stage is too small or there isn't enough backstage storage space. I hear about the lack of fall arrest systems. But the complaint I hear the most is the one about the lack of communication between the tour and the roadhouse. I hear about how the drawings never get read by the house staff. I hear about venue managers that don't know (or don't care) how much weight their roof systems can support.

Shows consistently get brought in to venues where the only measure of how much the roof can hold is how much was hung there before. I've heard "It's held everything we've ever put on it" far too often. And the touring companies aren't any better. Road crews frequently don't have a clue as to how much weight they're hanging from the roof steel. Or if they do offer a weight, it's often woefully underestimated.

And you know, everyone complains about the other guy on the other side. No one is taking responsibility for any of this. The road guys say it's the venue managers who are the problem and the venue managers blame the road guys. I'm not sure I care whose fault it is, but I do know it needs to get fixed. It's a good bet that if things stay this way, our luck is going to run out and someone is going to get killed.

Listening to all the complaining gets me thinking that some folks just aren't learning. If you've experienced a problem in the past, and you haven't done anything to correct it, then you can assume it will continue in the future unless you actually do something to correct the situation. Your drawings aren't being read by anyone in the venues you're playing? Then send the drawings earlier and bug the hell out of the venue managers until they either read the drawings or admit they don't have anyone on staff that knows how.

And please make sure the drawings are accurate. There's not much worse (at least in this context) than finally getting someone to read the drawings you've sent only to discover that they're wrong. That center truss that you guessed at 1,500 pounds but came in at 1,900? It may not seem like a big deal to you, but discrepancies in the field make venue owners and managers very nervous. If you lose someone's trust it takes a long time, and hard work, to get it back.

The shows are getting larger, the budgets are getting tighter and the venues aren't getting any younger. Just because that place you played last year held 75,000 pounds doesn't mean that it will hold 80,000 this year. Get the lines of communication open as early as possible and keep them open. Yes, I know things change on a moment's notice. Designers wait till the last minute to decide what wiggle light they want to use and the producers aren't always sure what cities they are going to be in until they get the show rolling. It makes it difficult but it doesn't make it impossible.

Of course the need for good communications doesn't stop just because you've finished planning and designing a show. No siree. You've still got load-in, tech rehearsal and the actual running of the show to deal with and to be successful you have to keep up the flow of information throughout.

As early as 2003 I had a cell phone that worked in Europe and the USA. Scientists have discovered a radio signal coming from elebenty-seven light years away that operates at a frequency so low no one can hear it. Whales can sing to each other over thousands of miles of ocean.

Now, if all of that long-range communication is possible, why is it so damned hard to get two people who are working on the same show in the same theatre at the same time to talk to each other? Sometimes it looks like we go out of our way to avoid discussing even the basic necessities of the show. I mean people need to know what's going on to do their jobs properly, right? But the following scenario gets played out, in one variation or another, over and over again in theatres around the country.

It's load in time at the local university theatre and it's a mad house onstage. Students stage right, students stage left. Students on the loading bridge and students – well, you get the idea. There's this full stage wall that has to get flown on a single pipe. There's also a border that needs to get hung to mask the hardware at the top of the wall. The wall goes on lineset eighteen and the border goes on lineset seventeen. The two pipes are flown in. The person in charge of the soft goods yells up to the bridge to get the border set properly weighted. Meanwhile the carpenter in charge of the scenery is also yelling up to get the wall set weighted. The crew people on the loading bridge are trying to be accommodating but, a) the loading bridge rail isn't numbered so the crew has to count from the proscenium to figure out which set they're supposed to be working on, b) they're not really happy to be that high and are feeling just a tad nervous, and c) it's really hard to hear up there because the air compressor is on so the carpenters can make some last minute alterations.

The end result is that the wrong set gets loaded and the counterweight arbor goes crashing to the floor, spilling weights all over the place.

I watched once as the high steel rigger on a concert rig went back to check the basket on a one-ton hoist point. The hoist was connected to a lighting truss and both the truss and the hoist were on the floor. The rigger discovered a problem with the point so he disconnected it to straighten it out. This, in and of itself, shouldn't have been a problem. However, at the same time the point was disconnected the road guy on the deck plugged in the hoist control and started to raise the truss. From here on everything went into slow motion. The rigger started yelling. The road guy was looking around trying to see what/where the problem was. To add to the confusion people were running across the arena floor flapping their arms trying to get his attention so he would stop running the hoist. He finally did stop, but by this time the truss was several feet off the floor. Meanwhile, overhead, the point was still disconnected save for the rigger hanging on as best he could. He had, in reality, become part of the bridle leg. This story had a happy ending. It all got straightened out and no one got hurt. (It was only later when the rigger was getting changed that he noticed his right sleeve was now longer than his left. Or was it?)

It would be one thing if accidents were isolated incidents, but they happen all the time. Maybe not in front of a few million TV viewers, but they happen in theatres and arenas all over the country.

The inability to communicate quickly and effectively has been the bane of the entertainment business for a very long time. How often, when asked why something went wrong, is the response, "I thought he said…" or, "I didn't understand," or, my personal favorite, "Nobody told me to/not to."

Part of getting a project completed is insuring that the lines of communication are direct, clear and firmly established. In a theatre during a load-in there should be one person on the deck who is in charge. That person, and only that person, should be talking to the crew on the loading bridge. And yes, there should be one person on the bridge who is in charge there. These two people are responsible for their areas and control everything that happens in them.

The same holds true for the arena shows. Granted, arena shows tend to be a bit larger but the principle is the same. One deck chief should be in charge of the overall load-in, and supervisors in charge of the various areas. The layout of the show and the venue determine how those areas are defined. The 26th Street Armory in New York City typically requires two deck chiefs, one at each end of the room. The Super Dome needs more.

Something else that needs a bit of refining is the method of communication. Screaming at the top of your lungs is not going to cut it in the Super Dome and everyone knows it. The production crew always brings in radios. But somehow that same crew will think that when they are in another venue with a roof at 100 feet they no longer need the radios. They would be wrong. A misunderstanding at 100 feet can be just as deadly as the one at 250 feet, or at 45 feet. Sailors in the seventeenth century knew that yelling wasn't very effective; that's why they had whistles. (Hence the superstition about whistling backstage.) This being the twenty-first century, we get electricity and radios. To have these tools at our disposal and not use them is just plain silly.

And then there's the speed thing. Bad communications only get exacerbated when the push is on. Go ahead. Tell me you've never heard "Hurry up, get that piece weighted, we've got another twelve to do and there's a rehearsal in fifteen minutes." Or how about, "The last point you hung is in the wrong place, get up there and fix it right away. The client will be here in just a few minutes."

My experience tells me that there are three main reasons for accidents in our industry – poor communications, lack of time and bravado. Whoever invented the phrase "the show must go on" didn't give a rat's patootie about the technicians working backstage. Yeah, I know. Actors work very hard and yes, it's difficult to perform in front of people without proper rehearsals. But it's the crew putting the show together without enough time and too little sleep who are the ones most at risk. Google some studies on sleep deprivation or the effects of working on extended overtime. You'll find one report after another that describes just how badly people perform mental and physical tasks when they haven't had enough sleep. Many report a significant loss of ability after ten hours. And that is with breaks. How many of you have gone twelve, fourteen or sixteen hours (or more) without a break? (Standing up at the catering table and wolfing down some lunchmeat in five minutes and then going back onto the truss does not constitute a break.)

News item. May 6, 2004. Stagehand falls to his death at David Bowie show in Miami. Mr. Wally Thomas was wearing a harness, but he was not clipped to the safety line.

Why do accidents like this happen? In the last few years there have been several fall-related fatalities where the worker was either not wearing the gear or wasn't connected to the safety line properly. In this day and age, what with all the information available out there, you would think we'd have a handle on this by now.

Which brings us to bravado. Bravado comes in many forms. There's the "it can't happen to me" type. That's the guy who climbs without a safety harness because, as he says, "I ain't gonna fall cause I ain't gonna let go." And then there's the "we don't have enough time and I know this shortcut" type. Being unwilling or unable to tell someone that there isn't enough time to do a particular job safely is an example of bravado gone wrong. So what's up with this? Why do we succumb to that "show must go on" crap?

Why do we load a heavy rig into a building when we haven't a clue how much the roof steel will hold because someone else (the structural engineer) didn't do his job? And why oh why, in this enlightened day, do we continue to flex our muscles and pretend that we're invincible? Because most of the time we get away with it, that's why. And getting away with it feels pretty good. Go ahead. Tell me I'm wrong.

Staying up all night and finishing that killer focus can be a real rush. There's an acute sense of accomplishment when it all magically comes together. Let's face it, we're adrenaline junkies. We go for that high of accomplishing something under great stress and against all odds. (It's important to remember that the four gallons of Red Bull you drank through the night may also have something to do with that feeling.)

And who needs to know what's going on anyway? We've been there, done that and know how to solve any problem that might come up so why waste time talking about it. If we didn't get it right the first time, then we'll fix it in the mix.

But then something like what happened to Wally Thomas comes along and we all get a dose of reality. It's not every day that someone is killed in this line of work, so it gets some airtime, at least for a little while. We post notices on websites; we talk about it in chat rooms and in emails. It gets a splash in the trade mags. But then it's gone. Time to move on to the next wiggle light show or big truss rig.

The idea is to make the lesson stay with us longer. As the saying goes, if we don't learn from our history then we are doomed to repeat it

We don't do such a bad job of staying safe in this business, but we need to do better. No one wants to hear about a friend taking a dive off a lighting truss or getting smacked in the head by a shackle pin falling from sixty-five feet. No one wants the phone call with the news that a son or daughter is in an ER a thousand miles away.

The question is how. How to stop the serious accidents without totally compromising the work? I have some suggestions. The first is the hardest. Learn how to say "no." When some fool boss asks you to work fourteen hours straight with no breaks, tell him "no." Tell him that it is illegal for him to require you to do something that is illegal or dangerous. And working those kinds of hours without proper breaks, and I mean real meal and sleep breaks, is dangerous.

And those people who take unnecessary risks – the ones who do stupid stuff like climb without the right gear or without clipping in? Talk to them. Make it known that you don't want to watch them do a headplant. Remind them just how damn easy it is to make a mistake and what the results may be. You don't want to be the one thinking, after something has gone terribly wrong, "I should've done something."

And finally, make time to get some more training. Nobody knows it all, and we all need refresher courses from time to time. Take advantage of the people and organizations out there in the real world who are doing what they can to train folks in the fine art of working and staying alive in the entertainment business. Check with your IATSE (International Alliance of Theatrical Stage Employees) local or with your workplace to find out what kinds of programs are available. If they don't have anything, then make enough noise until they do. Take some outside classes or help your employer find a trainer to bring in-house. It may take a little digging to find the program that's right for you, but they're out there. Considering the alternative, the search is worth it. Here are a couple of options to investigate.

Rigging Workshops. There are a number of individuals and organizations taking an interest these days in training. They usually set up in a hotel or theatre somewhere and advertise the session dates in the trade magazines. These workshops tend to be three- to five-day intensive sessions replete with hands-on work and gobs of literature.

Hire-in Workshops. Some companies will bring a training session to your theatre or shop. The sessions are designed specifically for your faculty and staff and typically last from one to three days.

Academic Courses. There may not be a lot of them, but they're definitely out there, on the college level and in vocational/technical schools around the country. Most theatre departments require not only classroom time, but production work too. This is a great way to get the basics and put them in practice.

For whatever it's worth, I suspect most of us like seeing our names in the paper. We're all looking for a little recognition, and a little publicity on occasion is good for the soul. Providing, of course, that the publicity is about something positive. Rescuing someone's grandmother from a burning building, for example, or hosting a charity event in your theatre. But having your stage roof collapse and injure or kill a few people is definitely not going to generate a positive image.

In the end, it's about the basics. Good lines of communication, accurate information and proper training will go a long way toward helping you get your name in the paper for all the right reasons.

Tools of the Trade

It's that time in the program when we open up a discussion on hardware. It's that stuff all around you all of the time. The nitty-gritty, nuts, bolts and shackles kind of stuff – without which we'd all be working in the props department. Now, maybe you know all about this stuff and maybe you don't. Only one way to find out and that's to grab a cup of coffee, put your feet up and read on.

Examining Rope

When I say "rope" some people may still think manila rope, the organic material we used for umpteen years before the synthetics came into vogue. After all, we still call theatres that have rope and sandbag rigging "hemp houses." Well, it's time to wake up and feel the splinters. Like it or knot (sorry) synthetic ropes are here to stay.

So settle in and learn a little about these new-fangled inventions called "rope."

There are three basic types of synthetic rope used in the entertainment industry. They all have the same fundamental properties because they are all made from the same base fiber, namely polyester. They're not affected by changes in humidity (or an accidental release of the deluge curtain). They all feel pretty good in your hands. After manila, how could they not? And they all knot well and resist abrasion. The differences between them are in their construction styles and their respective working load limits.

The first and most popular is a composite rope that has a three-strand twisted construction. The construction style may sound a bit sinister but trust me, it's a very benign rope and stage technicians like it a lot. To make the rope the folks at the factory first take many strands of fiber and twist them into a bundle. Then they take three of those bundles and twist them around each other. The end result is a rope that looks a lot like manila but guess what? No splinters!

It's called a composite rope because it's actually made of two different fibers. In addition to polyester, it also has polyolefin. (Try saying that word three times fast). The manufacturer adds the polyolefin to the polyester to inexpensively build a large diameter rope, like the ¾" we typically use in a counterweight system. The polyolefin, however, has no strength rating; it really is just a filler material.

The end result is a rope that works very well in a counterweight system. It's very easy to spike a trim mark properly and it doesn't cost a lot of money. To properly "spike a trim mark," by the way, you need to twist open the rope and insert a length of colored cloth ribbon so that at least ½" of both ends of the ribbon are visible. My preferred method is to use a chopstick to push the ribbon through the line.

But there is a small drawback to this rope. Using the polyolefin as filler results in a strength reduction in the rope. The working load limit (WLL) of ¾" diameter rope, using a 7:1 design factor, is approximately 1,500 pounds. Tying a knot in the rope, as you do when you tie it to the counterweight arbor, requires a further reduction (50%, on average) of that WLL. So, ultimately, your three-strand twisted rope has an effective WLL of just 750 pounds.

Another rope commonly found in counterweight systems is the parallel core rope. This rope is made from 100% polyester fibers and has an interesting construction. It has a shell and a core. The shell is made of braided polyester, which is very nice on the hands. The shell is braided and its job is to encapsulate the core and protect the core from damage. The core is made up of lots and lots of fibers running alongside each other; hence the name parallel core. The rope is built this way to cut down on stretch as much as possible, and it works. It also has a decent working load limit. Three-quarter inch diameter parallel core rope has a WLL of 2,514 pounds. This rope is stronger than the three strand twisted, even after calculating the 50% reduction for the knots.

Finally, we have the double braid. (No, I'm not talking about a Scandinavian hairstyle.) This one is made up of a core, which is braided, and a shell, which is also braided. This type of construction makes for a great all-purpose, flexible, blue-collar kind of rope. (Sort of the Chevy of the rope family.) We use this rope as a general rigging work line, to lift that barge, tote that bale and haul a chain hoist to the grid. It's also used as the tackle part of block and tackles, and in rope (which used to be known as "hemp") houses. Here are the whys and wherefores.

This rope is extremely flexible and very strong (the WLL of ⅝" diameter is 1,571 pounds). You can drag it around on the floor for a while, drive a forklift over it, and generally still use it to haul gear in the air.

You can get it with practically any tracer color you want. Think about that for a second. In a rope (formerly "hemp") house with a five-line set, you had to fight your way through the bundle trying to find the short center line so that you could trim the damn set. Meanwhile the short line and the long, long line took a stroll to Vegas, got married, and now the whole thing is out of whack – big time. The road carpenter is none too happy with you either. Now imagine, instead of all that fancy handwork, all you had to do was yank on the line with the blue tracer, *et voila!* A perfectly trimmed set! You're happy, the roadie is happy, and the short and long, long lines have avoided a relationship that would have undoubtedly ended in a nasty divorce.

This rope is authorized and warranted for use in our industry. That means that the manufacturers actually know what we do with their ropes and they say it's okay. This comes in handy down the road should there be a problem.

The downside to double braid is that it is difficult to spike with a trim mark, as the outside shell will milk, or slide, over the core. This makes its use as a counterweight purchase line a definite no-no.

So in summary, for a counterweight set use either the three-strand line or the parallel core line, depending on your strength requirements and the depth of your pockets. For all of your other rope needs (and the mind boggles at the possibilities) use the double braid.

And remember, the rabbit comes out of the hole, goes around the tree seven or eight times, then gives up and goes to McHale's for a beer. (Regretfully, McHale's – the famous stagehands' bar in New York City – was torn down last year.)

Wire Rope and Aircraft Cable

Okay. Now we get to look at wire rope. It's great stuff, worth its weight in, well, steel. The world is full of many different types of wire rope: right regular lay, right lang lay, left lang lay, rotation resistant. You get the idea. There are many different types of wire rope for the many different applications out there in the real world. The entertainment business, in general, uses one particular kind. And that would be 7 x 19 galvanized aircraft cable.

Wire rope types are named according to their construction. 7 x 19 means that there are seven bundles of wires and each bundle has nineteen strands. Aircraft cable is further recognizable because it has a center, or core. We use 7 x 19 because it works the best for most theatre applications (What did you expect me to say? Because it's pretty?!?) and because it's relatively inexpensive.

And now the rules. A couple of don'ts, a few dos, and you're on your way.

Don't tie the aircraft cable into knots. It may kink or break. The only people I know who tie knots in cable are circus riggers and the Flying by Foy people. Have you ever seen a circus knot? Looks like something the cat horked up. The Foy folks swear by it. I swear too every time I come up against one of those babies during a strike. Bring out the C-7s! (Peter Foy used to get livid when he heard people call it a Foy knot. He didn't invent it and he refused to teach anyone outside of his shop how to tie it. So unless you have worked for Peter or the circus, I'd stay away from it.)

Don't grease or oil the cable. It doesn't need it and if the cable rubs up against your clothes you'll have a stain even your mom can't get out. Grease on a length of cable attracts and holds grit like nobody's business. When the cable runs around a pulley wheel, the grit can get forced into the middle of the cable and start grinding against the cable strands. This will eventually break a few of those strands. And that will cause a break in the cable. Bad idea, that. So please. No grease, no oil, no WD-40, no nothing.

Do make sure the pulleys in the system are the right size for the cable diameter you are using. Do this by using the bending ratio, aka the D/d ratio. The D/d ratio says that you multiply the diameter of the cable by a number (the number varies depending on the type of cable) to get the proper diameter for the pulley. When using aircraft cable the minimum D/d number is 26. Most people I know use 32. This way you do not damage the cable as it passes around the pulley.

Do make sure that the cable, when running through a pulley sheave, is centered in the groove of that sheave and enters and exits the sheave in a straight line. If the cable runs more than 1½ degrees off the centerline of the sheave groove (this is called a fleet angle) you may damage the sheave and the cable.

Do use the right cable fitting for the job. So what are the right fittings, you ask? The ones that don't fail, I answer. Seriously though, we use cable clips and swage sleeves as our primary types of cable fittings. Both terminate cable nicely, thank you, but the methods of installing them are different. Let's start with swage sleeves since they are my personal favorites.

Cable Fittings

Swage sleeves compress around the cable by means of a special crimping tool. When applied correctly, a swage sleeve has an efficiency rating of 95 to 100%. This means that given the originally stated load rating of the cable before applying the sleeve, you still have 95 to 100% of that load rating after the sleeve is applied.

These sleeves are way cool because they are easy to install *and* have a high efficiency rating. But they do have a bit of a drawback. If you install a sleeve improperly or put it in the wrong place, the only way to remove it is to cut it off.

The only way to make sure that the sleeve has been installed properly is to check it with a Go/No Go Gauge. The gauge is a piece of metal plate with notches cut into it. You locate the notch that corresponds to the size of the sleeve you are crimping, and try to slip the notch over the sleeve. Please make sure that you are testing the area that you crimped, not the part between the crimps. If the gauge fits snugly over the sleeve, you're golden. If it doesn't fit, your crimping tool is in need of adjustment and the sleeve(s) should be replaced. Check the manufacturer's specs for tool adjustment.

There are two major manufacturers of swaging equipment in the United States. The National Telephone and Telegraph Co. in Cleveland, Ohio, which makes the Nicopress brand and the Loos Co. in Naples, Florida, which produces Locolok. It's important that you do not mix the equipment, tools or hardware from the two companies. The sleeves are not regulated and so they may not be exactly the same size from one company to another. In addition, the crimping tools are not identical. Nicopress, for example, requires three crimps per sleeve in some of the more common sizes while Locolock requires four. If you do mix the two companies' products together you run the risk of an inaccurate reading from the Go/No Go Gauge or, possibly, failure due to the wrong number of crimps.

I have discovered that a lot of sleeves are being used out there in the real world, but not a lot of gauges. Who has the time to check sleeves when supper's on the table? You do! A piece of advice: make sure that there is a Go/No Go Gauge attached to your crimping tool. Use it whenever you begin a new job, and, on the bigger projects like rigging system installations, every fifty crimps. Check with your supplier and/or manufacturer about gauges, tools or any other questions you might have.

Now, up to the plate, batting cleanup, are wire rope clips. There are two types of wire rope clips: drop-forged and malleable. Both have a U-bolt and saddle assembly that requires a wrench to attach. The difference between the two lies in the manufacturing process. Drop-forged is the harder and stronger of the two. When applied correctly, cable clips have an efficiency rating of 80%. (Pop quiz: What's the efficiency rating of swage sleeves?)

Wire rope clips, like swage sleeves, have their pluses and minuses. Clips can be removed more easily than swage sleeves. You do not need a gauge to determine that the installation has been done correctly. And you can see inside the clips. (Some people don't trust swage sleeves because they can't actually see what's going on inside the fitting. Here's a question for you folks in particular: Do you look inside the head gasket every time you start your car?)

On the downside, these clips are very often put on backward. You've heard the expression, "Never saddle a dead horse," right? That means that you do not put the saddle of the clip onto the dead end (tail) of the wire rope. If you do, then the U-bolt is on the load bearing part of the line and is merrily crushing the wire rope beneath it. This is probably the most common mistake I see when I conduct safety inspections. The result of this boo-boo is that you've lowered the efficiency rating to somewhere around zero. Not a good idea.

Installing wire rope clips is a two-step process. Once you have tightened the clips the first time to the correct torque setting (for ¼" clips the torque is 15 foot pounds) you have to then apply a significant load to the line. Adding the load will stretch the cable a bit and the diameter of the wire rope becomes a teensy bit smaller. This allows the clips to loosen up, if only just a little. So then you go back and tighten the clips again. Finally, wire rope clips need regular maintenance. The torque setting should be checked annually. This is one of the reasons I prefer swage sleeves.

Hardware Considerations

Question: When is a turnbuckle not a turnbuckle?
Answer: When someone forgets to mouse it and it unscrews itself. (Think about it.)

Okay, I'll come right out and tell you that I do not like turnbuckles. Not in rigging systems anyway. These babies were designed for static loads. You know, like holding up plaster ceilings or tensioning guy-wires on telephone poles. (Remember when phones had wires?) Turnbuckles were not designed for live (moving) loads. The main problem is that cutting the threads on the turnbuckle bolt makes those bolts somewhat brittle. So if something hits them, they can bend pretty easily. Once metal bends it's not too long till it breaks.

Another problem with turnbuckles is that you can put a lot more force on a turnbuckle than you might realize. One of the things I have seen people do when tightening turnbuckles is to whip out a handy dandy adjustable wrench, stick the handle into the body of the turnbuckle, and then tighten. Baaaad idea. When you tighten the turnbuckle with another device, like a wrench, you can place more force on the turnbuckle than it was designed to hold. You could also place too much force on the item (aircraft cable, for example) you are trying to tension. Too much force and the cable could break. A cable snapping is a dangerous thing. The broken end of the cable will come whipping right back at you with astonishing force. Trust me. You don't want to be in the same time zone with a piece of cable, rope, whatever, when it breaks. There is much pain and blood involved. So, when you are tightening up a turnbuckle, just do it by hand.

If I were you I'd try to avoid using turnbuckles on moving things, like pipe battens. If you use them to hang scenery make sure the turnbuckle is protected from smacking into something else and getting bent. Bury it into the back of the flat at the bottom, for example. And always, always, always safety (sometimes called "mousing") the turnbuckle with a piece of baling wire, a tie wrap or similar device to prevent the turnbuckle from twisting loose.

Can I talk about shackles now? Shackles are good. Shackles are our friends. Shackles are cool. (I obviously need to get a life.)

Shackles – screw pin anchor shackles to be precise – are the mainstay of the rigging business. If you have something to hang you may not always need a chain hoist but chances are you're gonna need a shackle.

A screw pin anchor shackle is made up of two parts. The larger part is called the bell. It's shaped a bit like an anchor, hence the name. On the open end of the bell there are two ears. Each ear has a hole in it; one threaded, one not. The other part of the shackle is the pin. It's a bolt. Sort of. It has threads on one end and a knob on the other. Screw the pin into the bell, and presto! – you have a working shackle.

When using a shackle the most important thing to remember is to always position the force (weight, load, whatever you want to call it) so that the force runs through the center axis of the shackle. Never allow a side load. Huh? Center axis?? Side load??? What the heck am I talking about, you ask? Reasonable questions. Here are the answers:

1. The center axis is the line drawn through the shackle running through the center of the pin and down through the center of the bell.

2. A side load occurs when the force is applied to the ears and not directly onto the pin or the round end section of the bell.

You want to avoid a side load because a side load force pulls against the ears of the bell and distorts the threads on the pin. Side loads cause a shackle to fail. So don't do it.

There are other things, of course, to remember about a screw pin shackle. One is that the blade (that knob on the end of the pin) has a hole in it. That hole has a purpose. It's there so you can prevent the pin from untwisting and falling out. Take some baling wire, a tie wrap or similar device, and run it through the hole and around the bell of the shackle as a safety. You want to do this *after* you have installed the shackle in to the system.

Another thing to remember is to never use a tool (like a screwdriver) to tighten the pin. This is a bad thing. (I can see some heads shaking at this point. You know who you are.) You should only tighten the pin with your fingers. When you use a tool you can over-tighten the pin and strip out the threads. You are also applying a load to the pin by over-tightening. This load can't be measured easily but is in addition to any actual weight you are hanging. If you tighten too much on an old pin and then hang a heavy load, you could be looking at a failure situation.

But the best reason to avoid using some kind of tool on the pin goes like this. If you use your fingers to tighten the pin when you set up a rig, but then need a tool to remove the pin after the show (as in, at strike) then there is something wrong with that shackle. It has been overloaded to the point where the threads have become jammed. The pin, my friends, is talking to you. (And you thought that was just any ol' voice in your head, didn't you?) It's saying, "Help me! Help me! I've been overloaded and I can't get out!" And what do we do with an overloaded shackle? We throw it out, that's what we do.

Curtain Track

No self respecting hardware chapter would be complete without a discussion of curtain track. Ask yourself this. Where would an actor be if he couldn't have a stagehand, standing offstage, opening and closing the act curtain for curtain calls? He'd still be onstage flailing around trying to find the center opening, that's where he'd be. Yes, it might be fun to watch from the wings, but the people out front wouldn't get it and you'd get yelled at. So we use traveler track.

There are two basic styles of track in the world: square steel type and aluminum I-beam type. There. That's all you need to know. If you understand this then you know everything there is to know about track, and I can go to the beach. See ya, bye!

What's that? I'm sorry I can't quite hear you. (The suntan lotion musta dribbled into my ears!) Did you say that I'm nowhere near finished with a track discussion? You think I should quit trying to weasel out of it, be a man for gosh (gosh?!?) sakes, and do the job right? (Sigh.) Well, okay.

There are two sizes of square type track and they are mostly used when curtains are doing straight runs. The larger of the two is heavy duty and cannot be curved. The smaller sized track is for medium weight stuff and, according to the manufacturers, can be curved – but only when the moon is in the second house, pigs fly, and my kids clean up their toys. Translation: it's possible to curve this track but it ain't fun.

The I-beam aluminum track also comes in two sizes and is more appropriate for use when you need to curve the track, like for a TV studio cyclorama. Now get this – the heavy duty I-beam track is for heavy duty curtains and such; the lighter track is for lighter stuff. What a concept, eh?

This story becomes slightly more interesting when you consider the hardware involved with track – especially if you're into hardware. I think the following little glossary of terms might give us a better shot at getting through all this.

Live End Pulley. This is the gizmo that is attached to the track over your head when you are trying to open or close the curtain. It has two pulleys in it; one to take the rope away from you, and the other to bring it back.

Dead End Pulley. This little pal is the pulley that turns the rope around at the other end of the track and sends it back toward you. Why it's called "dead end" I have no idea. Maybe it grew up on the wrong side of the tracks. (Sorry.)

Master Carrier. The master carrier is the trolley that the onstage edge of the curtain is attached to. It's called the "master" because it is also what the operating rope (see below) is attached to. All the other little carriers follow right along behind the master. Here's an analogy for you: a day care class in New York City out on a field trip. The leader of the class has a rope attached to him/her and then, in a nice little line behind, come all the cute little munchkins, all tied up so's they don't get lost. (It's particularly interesting getting these kids on the subway, as you can imagine.)

Single Carriers. These are those cute little kids following the master around. But unlike the day care example, these carriers are *not* attached to the operating rope, only to the curtain. There is a reason for this. The curtain has hooks that attach it to the carriers, which are usually 12" apart along the full length at the top. If the carriers were all attached to the rope every 12" you'd never be able to open the curtain. It wouldn't stack on the ends of the track. Think about it. Go ahead, take your time, I'll wait.

Operating Rope. This is a rope. You pull on it one way and the curtain opens. Pull the other way and it closes. Manually operated curtain ropes are often made of ½" diameter cotton rope with a synthetic center. The cotton makes it easy to grip and the synthetic core cuts down (somewhat) on the stretch.

Floor Sheave. This is the pulley that hangs down around the floor right where you want to stand when you are pulling the rope. It gets in the way and you're often tempted to toss it into the orchestra pit. Don't do that. Without that sheave, the rope coming down from the live end pulley will twist up faster than a phone cord in a teenager's hand the week before the prom. The sheave is also adjustable to help take out the slack when the rope stretches.

Okay, that's the basics of track hardware. Here's a drawing of a rigged bi-parting (opens in the middle) act curtain type track.

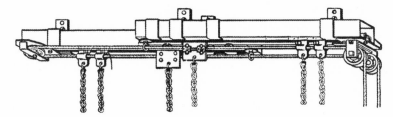

image courtesy of Automatic Devices Company

To rig this track start with both master carriers pulled as far to the middle as possible without hitting the end stops on the track. Estimate how long your operating rope needs to be. To do that you should add the track length to the curtain height, multiply by two and, just to be safe, add another ten feet. Take one end of the operating rope and tie it to the stage right side of the number one master carrier. Pull the rope stage right, through the live end pulley, down to the floor sheave below, then back up to the live end pulley. Wait, you're not done yet, the rope then goes across the stage, through the number two master carrier, into the dead end pulley and back out through the front. Now it goes back across the stage to the first master carrier. There, after you pull out all the slack, you should tie the rope to the stage left side of the first master carrier. Using the little U-bolt thingies you get with the master carriers, attach the rope to the second master carrier. You do not cut the rope here. Just put the bolts over the rope and clamp down. Ta-da! You've now rigged yourself a traveler track that operates from stage right! Reverse the process for stage left operation.

Now can I go to the beach?

-3-
Counterweight Systems

Over the years people have asked me for a little information on counterweight systems. You know, the pull-on-the-rope-and-the-scenery-goes-up-and-down stuff. No motors, no speed reducers or anything fancy. Perhaps this is because theatrical rigging system training has dropped off over the last decade or so in favor of the more esoteric chain hoist and truss training. And while chain hoist and truss training is extremely important, I believe it is equally important that the owners and operators of counterweight rigging systems also receive proper training. Counterweight systems have their own set of issues and are just as dangerous, if not more so. The gear in a counterweight system can be just as confusing as that in a convention center rig.

    I am going to assume that most of you know what loft blocks and head blocks are, but I think some other basic info might be in order. For those of you who know everything and are above a little refresher course, turn to the next chapter.

Owning a single purchase counterweight set does not mean that you only have to buy it once. It does mean that the pipe batten and the counterweight arbor have a one to one relationship. (Like me and Rudy, my dog!) When you pull on the operating line the arbor goes in one direction and the pipe goes in the other, and, like me and my dog, they both travel the same distance.

Getting the pipe to move correctly is where it gets tricky for some people. If you put something on the pipe batten – you know, lights, scenery, your mother in law – then you have to put some counterweight in the arbor. It's a good idea if the weight in the arbor equals the weight on the pipe. This keeps gravity in its place and allows the pipe to move up and down a lot more easily when you pull on the rope. When you're ready to take the lights or scenery off the batten, lower the batten to the deck first and remove the weights from the arbor. If the pipe is down and you remove the weights in the arbor, then the pipe stays down. If you leave the weights in the arbor – which is up at the loading bridge – and remove the lights, then gravity takes over and the arbor – with all the weights – comes crashing down. This is not a good thing.

We're going to continue our talk about loading the weights in a minute or so, but first let's take a look at your counterweight arbor guide system. I'm no rocket scientist, but I can bring you up to speed on the various guide systems in use in theatres these days.

Guide Systems

The object of a counterweight guide system is to make sure that the counterweight arbors go up and down smoothly and safely. It just won't do to have the arbors crashing into the loading bridge, the fly gallery or each other. It is considered very bad form when an arbor bangs into one of its neighboring arbors, lifts a counterweight off and sends the weight crashing to the floor. If you're lucky, the weight hits only the floor. A weight landing anywhere else could ruin someone's whole day. So let's talk about these systems in an attempt to avoid raining counterweight, shall we?

First up is the wire guide system. This system was designed as an inexpensive way to control arbors in small theatres. Each guide consists of two wires that run from the floor to the roof and run through holes in the top and bottom of the arbor. These holes are spaced so that the cables are in front and in back of the counterweight stack, leaving enough room to load and unload the weights.

The wire guides should be made of ¼" diameter galvanized aircraft cable. I say "should" because I've seen them made with everything from single strand guy wire to hemp to clothesline. Galvanized aircraft cable works best because it has some flexibility. It will give a little when the arbor moves up or down. The guy wire, especially the single strand stuff, is very brittle and has no stretch at all. If a kink develops in a guy wire, the wire will break in no time. The cable, because of its flexibility, is much less likely to kink or break.

By the way, the use of manila or cotton rope as guides is just plain silly. The holes through the arbor are not sleeved or protected in any way and the arbor plates will cut through a rope in short order. If you are in a theatre that's using fibrous rope as guide lines, please stop using the system until the lines are replaced with cable.

There should be a turnbuckle at the floor block connection point of the wire guides. This will allow you to tension the cable properly. Make sure you don't over-tighten the cable though. Never use a tool (like the handle of an adjustable wrench) in the body of a turnbuckle to tighten the turnbuckle. Tighten it by hand only.

I remember visiting a nearby university for a safety inspection. When I went looking in the normal place for the locking rail, it wasn't there. It seems the students had over-tightened the cables and pulled the entire rail out of the floor. The rail rose up and the battens came down until both were hanging at about the same height. It was pretty funny, but not terribly useful.

The other thing to remember about a wire guide system is that you should not use this system if your head block steel is more than thirty-five feet above the floor. Once you get past that height it becomes all but impossible to tighten the guide cables properly.

They'll just keep on stretching. Too much stretch and you get that bouncing into stuff thing going that we're trying to avoid.

And finally, make sure there are positive stops to limit the travel of the arbor. If there isn't a crash bar on the locking rail and at the head block, you must use properly sized stop sleeves. These are designed to stop the arbors when they have reached the end of their respective travel (psstt – that's why we call them stop sleeves – pass it on). Never use a cable clip in place of a stop sleeve. It really damages the cable and, if that's not enough, a clip will eventually slide as the arbor smacks into it during the run of a show. Once the clip slides it won't stop the arbor in the right place anymore. Where's the fun in that?

Okay. Enough about wire guides. How about T-bar? (A T-bone sounds better right now, but I gotta finish this section before I have dinner.) T-bar guide systems are used in larger theatres with larger numbers of counterweight sets, stacked closer together than traditional wire guide systems might allow. It is a much more rigid system. This means the rigging can be much taller than the thirty-five feet permitted by a wire guide system. Got a theatre with the head blocks at eighty feet? You better have a solid guide system to keep those arbors in line. Don't want those arbors wandering around, no sir.

A T-bar system is a series of vertical steel members that are, well, T shaped. The flat side (top of a T) is facing onstage and the bottom of the T is behind. The standard size is 1½" x 1½" x ³⁄₁₆" thick. The Ts run from the floor up to the head block steel and are usually spaced every six or eight inches. The Ts are built on a frame and the entire assembly is called a battery. In between each pair of Ts fit the guide plates (called shoes) of a counterweight arbor. These shoes are held captive in the Ts. This not only allows the arbor to run up and down smoothly but also keeps it from wobbling side to side. Pretty slick huh?

The nice thing about a T-bar system is that, when properly installed, it requires very little maintenance. You just have to go and tighten up some bolts every few years or so. The catch is that it isn't always installed properly. For the arbors to ride smoothly and easily, the T-bars have to be straight and plumb. They can't bend side to side or onstage/offstage. Bending creates friction and friction makes it harder to move the arbors. Think about it. Have you got a lineset that runs pretty easily until the arbor is two-thirds of the way up the wall? Does it become difficult to pull at that point for about ten feet? It's probably because the T-bar wasn't installed straight. Maybe a bolt was put into the wrong hole or missed the hole altogether. Maybe one of the wall plates on the frame wasn't adjusted properly. The best way to check for proper alignment of T-bar is to get above each one of the Ts (wearing fall arrest equipment, of course) with a good light and sight down the individual T. You'll be surprised at how easy it is to spot fluctuations in the run of each T. Once you've identified the problem, it becomes a matter of climbing down the T (with proper fall arrest equipment once again) and fixing it.

There is a common misconception that greasing a T-bar will help correct these problems. It won't. As the arbors run up and down, the grease builds up on top of the guide shoes. There it will sit, building up and building up until it becomes large enough to fall off (I suspect it leaps, actually). And when does it fall? When you are running the set and looking up, right? Right. And where does it land? C'mon, you know the answer to this one. Right in your eye, of course. Doesn't matter if you're wearing safety glasses or not, it will find a way. Plus, dust and dirt will stick to the surface of the grease and, over time, become thick enough to become a fire hazard. Anyone who has ever attempted to weld something to a T-bar guide and had it go off like a piece of flash paper knows from whence I speak. Another really good reason for not greasing the T-bar is that inspectors need (okay, like) to climb the T-bar while they are checking out a rigging system. The grease makes that a lot trickier.

Gaining in popularity is the aluminum J-bar system. A J-bar is a lot like a T-bar, except that is shaped like a J. No big surprise there. The surprise comes in that J-bar is normally made of aluminum. This may not mean a lot to you, the end user, but it sure means something to the installer. J-bar is a third the weight of steel Ts, making it a lot easier to ship and install. In operation, it is used the same as T-bar.

So there you have it. Keep your wire guides tight. Make sure your Ts and Js are straight and you're on your way to rigging heaven. Or at least a well running, safe system.

Loading and Unloading Arbors

Now, let's talk about those counterweight arbors. You know, the things that hold the weights? Counterweight arbors ("cradles" to our good friends in the UK) are a relatively simple, but essential, element of a manual rigging system. A counterweight arbor is a metal frame that rides in the guide track. It is where you put the steel weights (the counterweights) that balance out the load when you put something on the pipe (also called a batten). The three most important things to know when working with counterweight arbors are:

1. When to load weight into the arbor.
2. How to keep the weights in the arbor.
3. When to take the weights out.

Let's start off with getting the weights into the arbor. Just for giggles, assume you've just started loading a production of *Kiss Me Kate* into your local high school theatre, which is equipped with a full counterweight rigging system, including a grid and loading bridge.

The first thing you'll want to do is hang the onstage lighting. So you bring down the battens that have been designated for lighting. Lowering these battens causes the counterweight arbors to rise to the loading bridge. Next, get out your lighting plot, the lights and lots of minions (crew people). Send two minions to the loading bridge and keep the rest onstage to hang the lights. Once you have all the lights, hardware, cable, etc. hanging on a batten, calculate (notice I didn't say "guess") how much the pipe and all the gear weigh. (Take off your shoes and use your toes if you have to.)

When you know that amount, call up to the nice minions waiting patiently (i.e., napping) on the loading bridge and ask them to load counterweight into the arbor. If you have a single purchase counterweight system you'll load an amount equal to the weight on the batten. If you have a double purchase system, then the nice minions will have to load twice the weight on the batten. (They may not like hearing this part, but that's the way a double purchase system works.) When the loading is done, you should have a reasonably balanced counterweight set that can be raised or lowered by one person.

To unload the arbor when you are taking the show out, you simply reverse the process. Bring the batten to the deck but don't take the lights or scenery off. Not yet. First remove the weights from the arbor, then take off the lights and/or scenery. And remember that the batten also has weight. You will need to leave a few counterweights in the arbor to balance out the empty batten.

Now, let's chat about keeping those weights where they belong. There are two key pieces of hardware that help prevent the weights from coming out of an arbor.

The first are spreader plates. These are steel plates about 2" wide and roughly 14" long with two holes in them; one hole for each of the ¾" diameter arbor rods. These plates slide up and down on those rods. Their sole purpose in life is to prevent the arbor rods from bending in the event of an out-of-balance accident. Whoa! Hold on for a sec. What's an out-of-balance accident, you ask?

An out-of-balance accident is when the weight in the arbor is greater than the weight on the pipe, or vice versa. It happens when too much weight is put into the arbor, when the weights are put into the wrong arbor (hey, it happens) or when the scenery is removed too soon from the pipe. When one of these scenarios occurs, the heavier side of the system (either the batten or the arbor, depending on the problem) can come crashing down to the floor or go screaming up to the grid. Need visualization? Okay, how's this?

You are the deck chief. You just loaded 500 pounds of lights onto lineset number ten and have now asked the crew on the bridge to load 500 pounds of counterweight into the arbor for set ten. But the loading crew gets confused and loads 500 pounds into the arbor for set number eleven. There is nothing on the batten for set eleven to balance this new weight. At some point the rope lock for set eleven gives up and lets the rope run through. This allows the arbor to come crashing to the floor and the pipe to go crashing into the grid. Got the picture?

So, back to those spreader plates. They are designed to keep the arbor rods from bending. Without the plates, the force of the collision of the arbor against the bottom stop, combined with the weights crashing around, could turn the ¾" steel rods to spaghetti. With the rods all twisted, the weights could easily fall or be forced out of the sides of the arbor. This is a bad thing. Weights bouncing around the stage are a definite no-no. The plates hold the rods by being placed properly into the counterweight stack. There should be no more than 2' between plates in the arbor. So just before the loaders on the bridge start putting weights into the arbor, they have to lift these plates up to the top of the arbor out of the way. Then they start putting weights in. When the weight stack gets to be 2' high, they allow one of the plates to drop down on top of the weights. Then they continue putting weights into the arbor. (Yes, right on top of that first plate.) When they get another 2' of weights in, they let another plate come down on top of the stack. See how this works? The plates are stuck there in the stack and they hold the rods together.

The other extremely important items in the arbor are the weight hold-down collars. These collars are steel tubes that ride up and down the arbor rods. There's one on each rod. They have a threaded hole in them with a thumbscrew inserted into the hole. These collars exist to prevent weights from being forced off the top of the stack when the arbor crashes into the top stop. How could that happen? Well, here's one example.

Maybe the deck chief didn't calculate properly and there's not enough weight in the arbor to balance the load. But there is enough to allow two people to pull the arbor down, which they do. So the pipe is pulled out to trim and locked off. An hour later, the master electrician needs to bring that pipe in because there's a dead lamp he/she needs to replace, but the electrician doesn't know about the out-of-weight condition. The rope lock is opened. The pipe starts descending by itself because it is heavier than the arbor. At this point the master electrician says a bad word. The pipe moves faster and faster until the arbor crashes into the top stop bar. The force of the crash is more than enough to knock a weight or two off the top of the stack. That's where the collars come in. They're supposed to be on top of the very top weight with the thumbscrews tightened against the arbor rods. That's what keeps those weights from flying off.

The thumbscrews need only be finger tight to do their job. You don't have to get crazy about it and pull out your Leatherman to tighten them. If you are one of the unfortunate ones who doesn't have thumbscrews but maybe hex bolts or round head stove bolts, get rid of 'em and put in thumbscrews. Much easier.

If the arbor hits the top stop and the collars aren't tightened down, or are not there at all, then a weight is going to come off that stack. And if you thought a weight falling out the side of the arbor two to three feet off the ground was a bad idea, a weight falling from grid height can be absolutely lethal. The weight hold-down collars must be tightened down at all times. The loaders are not finished with their jobs until those collars are in place and tightened down.

And that, as they say, is that. Using the spreader plates and weight hold-down collars properly will not prevent runaway arbors. But it will certainly help minimize the damage and possible injuries caused by one of those accidents.

Floor Blocks and Slack in the Line

This is a good time to address a question I'm asked on occasion. In a T-bar or J-guide system, why does the floor block move up and down? Oh ye of so few years. Floating floor blocks were born in the age of organic operating lines. What we all called, with varying degrees of disgust, either manila or hemp.

Floor blocks moved for two reasons. The first reason, which is becoming outdated but is worth repeating, was to compensate for the elasticity of the rope. The organic ropes, you see, would stretch or shrink depending on the atmospheric conditions in the building. Less humidity in the air meant the lines would begin to dry out. When that happened the length of the rope increased. On the other hand, when the rope absorbed moisture, as in the summer time when it was more humid outside and there was less climate control inside, the rope shrank. To avoid placing undue stress on the rigging system and to keep proper tension in the operating line, the floor block was designed to float. The pressure placed by the line on the block was relatively even on both sides of the block, so the block would move easily. When the pressure on the block came from one side of the line or the other, as in when the lineset was being operated, the block would jam in the guide tracks. This reduced the slack in the line, which in turn allowed the operator to hit a trim mark accurately.

Slack in an operating line can create one of the more embarrassing moments in a production. It's the middle of the second act and you are lowering the backdrop during the quietest moment of the evening. You see the spike mark in the line approaching and prepare to stop the piece. But, unbeknownst to you, there is about six inches of extra play in the line. Consequently, the drop hits the floor before you reach the trim mark. This results in two sounds heard by the audience. The first is the drop's bottom stretch pipe hitting the floor with a thud. The second is you muttering under your breath, "*Sh*t*." (It is impossible to whisper the word sh*t. No matter how hard you try to cover, it still carries to the back of the house.)

Another reason for a sliding floor block is that there are times when slack in the operating line is helpful. When installing a twenty-five-foot tall full stage traveler curtain, it can be difficult to properly balance the weight. The curtain is laid out on the stage, the batten is brought in and the top of the curtain is tied off to the pipe. The curtain weighs 350 pounds, so the next task would be to place 350 pounds of weight in the counterweight arbor. This presents a problem, however. The curtain may weigh 350 pounds but that weight isn't really applied to the rigging system until the curtain is up off the floor and hanging in the air. Adding weight to the arbor while the curtain is on the floor places a strain on the system. The weights being added are trying to force the arbor down. To combat this force a snub line is tied around the operating lines and back to the locking rail before the additional weight is installed. The snub line holds the operating line and allows the operator to get out of the way while the weights are being placed in the arbor.

To properly install a snub line requires slack in the operating lines. To achieve some slack in the operating lines requires a floating floor block. While pulling up on the offstage line you push down on the front of the block with your foot. There's a toe clip there for this very reason. The block slides up and you are now holding at least a foot of slack in your hands. Twist the front and back operating lines together as much as the slack will allow and then tie the snub line. Now the weights can be added, the operator is safe and control of the system is maintained even when it is out of balance. You wouldn't have been able to do that if the floor block wasn't able to slide.

Rope Locks

Next we come to the rope lock. That's the device that you bump into along the rail; the thing with the long handle that moves up and down and usually gets in the way. The truth about rope locks is this: The sole function of a rope lock is to prevent a counterweight line set from moving when it's not supposed to.

When I do theatre safety inspections I get to see a lot of, well, interesting problems. While I've seen a number of really oddball rigs, there are some consistent problems that show up in almost every inspection. I'd like to address one of these common problems so that hopefully you can learn something and start fixing it before I have to write another report that includes: "Rope locks need adjustment."

Here's the way the rope lock works. The operating rope of a counterweight system runs through the housing of the lock. Inside that housing are two smooth curved metal pieces called dogs. When you raise the handle on the rope lock, the front (onstage) dog is pushed up against the rope. This is done by a metal bump (cam) on the rope lock handle. Lower the handle and you release the dog, thereby releasing the rope. You do not need the Army Corps of Engineers to adjust this lock. You can do it yourself. If you want to adjust how much pressure the dogs place on the rope, there is a thumbscrew and nut assembly on the back of the lock housing. The thumbscrew pushes the offstage dog in and out thereby opening or closing the hole that the rope runs through.

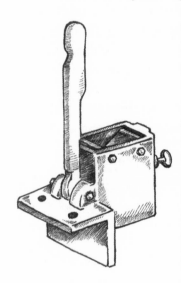

So why, you ask, if we are using a counterweight system where everything is supposed to be balanced, do we need a rope lock at all? It is not, regretfully, a perfect world out there. Nor is a counterweight set an exact science. Counterweights are manufactured in 1" and 2" thicknesses that are about twelve and twenty-four pounds each, respectively. You can get close to balance with those weights, but not perfect. Under normal conditions you can be out of weight by a half weight and not be able to get any closer to being balanced. The rope lock compensates for that imperfection.

You will notice that I have been calling these devices rope "locks" throughout this section. Not once have I referred to them as rope brakes. That's because they ain't brakes. (A hushed silence fills the room.) Rope locks, you see, are designed to hold, not stop, a set from moving. If you engage the lock while the rope is running, the dogs can, over time, severely damage the rope due to the friction (i.e. heat) and abrasion created by the rope running against the dogs. Unlike the rope lock you, who have eyes, ears and a brain, get to be the rope stopper before the piece runs through that lovely little baby grand piano onstage.

There's another thing I'd like to pass on concerning these locks. There are several people (consultants, architects and other intelligent types) out there who swear up and down that the rope locks are capable of holding up to 200 pounds. And that they should always be adjusted to do just that. This means that a lineset could, in theory, be out of weight by as much as 200 pounds and you might not know it. All of you who weigh less than 200 pounds, please pay attention to this next part. What happens if you, being the diminutive type weighing in at 145 pounds, open up a rope lock on a set which, unbeknownst to you, is out of balance by 200 pounds? You go for a ride on the operating line, that's what happens.

If you aren't paying strict attention when you open an out of balance set, it'll pull you off your feet. Human nature, contrary to what they may tell you in school, can be silly sometimes. Every story I have ever heard of someone being pulled off his or her feet by an out of weight set started off with, "I don't know what I was thinking. I grabbed on to the rope harder instead of letting go!" And then, off you go! The first thing you'll encounter is usually the index strip light pipe – with your shoulder. That may slow you down a bit, but it probably won't stop you. Next comes the loading bridge with its big ol' channel support frame. That'll stop you. And guess what? Now is when you will let go. If this sounds like I'm speaking from experience – you betcha. Trust me, this is not nearly as much fun as a good roller coaster ride at Busch Gardens.

Guess what happens when the set is pipe-heavy by 200 pounds? This time you get strained through the rope lock like a Playdough Fun Factory.

So here's the deal. Your rope locks should be able to hold a counterweight set that is out of balance by up to forty to forty-five pounds, but no more than that. At that weight, you are not damaging the rope when you pull up on the handle, and even if you aren't paying attention, you can handle that much weight without assistance. To judge what forty to fifty pounds feels like, here are two tests you can do.

1. Raise and lower the rope lock handle with one hand. If you can lock it and open it with a medium amount of difficulty, you should be okay. If you need to use a four-foot piece of pipe as a lever arm (and yes, I've seen this done a zillion times) over the handle, then it's too tight. If you need a Chuck Norris type side kick to lock the handle, it's also too tight.

2. Knowing that the set is in balance, raise the handle into the locked position. Place your feet flat on the floor and grab the rope just above the lock. Now pull up with all you've got. If you can move the rope just a little bit, you're doing fine. If you can't move it at all, it's too tight or if you can pull it up one handed, it's too loose.

One final note about weights and minor out-of-balances. As the scenery piece is lowered, the weight from the cable lift lines is transferred from the arbor side to the loft block side and vice versa when the piece is raised. That's why things tend to move faster when they get closer to the ends of their travel distances.

And so, my friends, you see that owning and running a counterweight system takes a lot of work and high degree of skill. This work is definitely not for beginners, at least, not by themselves. Make sure you get proper training before you operate these systems. If you're in school then that training should come in the beginning stages of your college career. If not, then maybe you could get to one of the seminars that are offered at various times around the country.

-4-
Fall Protection

It's fascinating to look back and see how safety awareness in our industry has evolved. (Yeah, I know. If I find that fascinating I'd better get out more often, huh?) In the '60s and '70s we didn't think much about safety. It wasn't hip to wear a safety harness when working overhead. We thought we were immortal. We thought we were cool.

Then the shows started getting bigger. The loads we were lifting got heavier. The arenas got larger. We needed more gear. (Remember when a forty-hoist show was considered big?) The more stuff we put in the air, the greater the opportunity for an accident. The '80s brought us more and more reports of injuries and deaths, many due to falling. It began to dawn on some of us that showboating wasn't such a great idea after all.

The rock climbers among us brought their sit harnesses, the ones they used while scampering around cliff faces, for work in the high steel. It seemed like a good idea at the time. Turned out it wasn't. The design was, and is, all wrong for the kind of work we do. If you took a fall in one of these harnesses you could do more damage to yourself than you wanted to think about.

You see, the problem was that we had no real information coming from anyone (manufacturers, engineers, safety specialists, etc.) as to what kind of gear worked and what didn't. We operated in the time honored theatrical tradition of trial and error. If it worked once, we kept using it till it stopped working. Then we moved on to something different. That works for a loose pin hinge. It's a lousy idea for a harness.

Eventually the Feds did take notice. The folks at OSHA (Occupational Safety and Health Administration) finally determined that there was a problem and that only they could solve it. So they developed some codes and regulations, rearranged some existing stuff and, amazingly enough, came up with a fall arrest system that actually works. (Now wrap your head around that one for a minute. A federal agency makes an attempt at being helpful and actually succeeds. Go figure.) The equipment that OSHA requires us to use will protect us from serious injury or death in the event of a fall.

So, compliments of Uncle Sam, we have a working fall arrest program for use in the entertainment industry. But even with these regulations it seems like the frequency of fall-related accidents is not declining. I conducted an informal and unscientific survey to see if I could get a hint as to what was going on and the results were not encouraging. The number of serious injuries and fatalities over the last ten years may actually have gone up. I discovered that there have been a number of reports – some official, some not – of people getting hurt because they were using the wrong type of fall arrest equipment, were using the right gear incorrectly or simply weren't wearing safety equipment.

I've also learned that there are still venue managers who either don't understand the way a fall arrest system is supposed to work or are simply ignoring the rules. There are theatres with loading galleries that have no railings and no horizontal lifelines. Crews are showing up for rigging calls at the local arena and there isn't a harness to be found in the building. And when the right equipment is provided there is no training on how to wear it properly. The OSHA regulations require your employer to not only supply the proper fall arrest equipment, but also to train you in the proper use of that equipment. These are good rules here folks. You should be paying attention to them.

You wouldn't dream of letting your seventeen-year-old son or daughter drive a car that didn't have working brakes. And you'd make sure he or she knew how to drive, right? Right. But you'll walk a truss without a harness on. Or you'll take the harness that the road guy tosses you and wear it even if you don't how to put it on. Having someone point at a harness in the road box and say, "Put this on," does not constitute training. A qualified person must show you how to wear the harness and how to connect it to the rest of the system.

How do I know who's qualified, you ask? The OSHA Standard 1926.32 (m), from Subpart C of Part 1926, "Safety and Health Regulations for Construction" has this to say:

"Qualified" means one who, by possession of a recognized degree, certificate, or professional standing, or who by extensive knowledge, training, and experience, has successfully demonstrated his ability to solve or resolve problems relating to the subject matter, the work, or the project.

Just as important as knowing what equipment to wear and how to wear it, you also have to know where you will need it. If you are in a place where you can fall more than six feet and there are no railings or other devices in place to protect you from falling, then you need a fall protection system. A classic example of an area in the theatre where you probably need fall protection is on the loading bridge. (Now just because you don't have a loading bridge, don't feel that you can skip over this part. The next theatre you work in may have one!) Assuming that you do have a loading bridge, you probably have railings on the onstage side and nothing (or maybe a skinny old piece of chain) on the offstage side. When someone is on this bridge to add or remove counterweights, fall protection is required.

Another area that commonly requires fall protection is the front of house catwalks and lighting positions. It's the same deal as the loading bridge. If you have no railing when you are hanging lights, or if you remove the railing when you need to hang or strike the instruments, then you must have fall protection. When you are doing those twenty-foot-tall box booms and the only way to get around is to climb the side arms, put on fall protection!

Use fall protection when using a focus track. Do you want to fall on your butt when the chair track fails, or would you prefer to be left hanging in a quasi-comfortable position until someone could get to you? Your choice.

There are a zillion other places in the theatre that you might need fall protection. And another gazillion on a rock 'n' roll touring show. I'm not even going to begin to try and list them all here. Follow the six foot rule, gang.

What we need to talk about next is the equipment. Here are some of the basic components:

1. An OSHA-compliant full body harness.
2. An approved lanyard, no longer than
   six feet, with a shock absorber.
3. A lifeline.
4. An anchorage point.

In addition, there are plenty of accessories and site-specific equipment on the market today, as safety has finally become big business. It's important to remember, however, that to be OSHA-compliant the equipment must meet or exceed an ANSI code and the label must identify that code. The most common codes used today are A10.32-2004 and Z-359-2007, which consists of five sections (.0 - .4). The theory here is that the equipment is in place to catch you when you fall. It does not prevent the fall. So how does the equipment work? Well, first you fall (yikes!). Then the full body harness is engaged and takes the load. The ring on the back of the harness slides up a bit providing some shock absorption. Then the lanyard, and more importantly, the shock absorber see the load. Finally, whatever forces are left – and there are *plenty* – are transferred to the lifeline and its anchorage points. So you see, the whole system is only as strong as the weakest element in it. So you better be damned sure that the weakest link is strong enough to support you should you fall. For a basic guideline, try this on for size:

Fall protection must be used as a complete system. All components of that system must be equal to the combined capabilities of that system. All components of the system must have a tensile strength of at least 5,000 pounds. (Hefty stuff!)

In English that means that the components of the system, along with the connections between the parts and the connection to the building, must each have a tensile strength of at least 5,000 pounds. It won't help if you have a working fall arrest system in place and then attach it to the building with a paper clip. (More on that in a minute.)

Let's do the easy stuff first. The harness. Harnesses must be the full body type with a sliding D-ring in the upper back for attachment to the next part of the fall protection system. And, surprise, surprise, it must be OSHA-compliant and be so labeled. Sit/climbing harnesses, which used to be very popular among rock 'n' roll riggers, are not acceptable substitutes. These harnesses may feel more comfortable as a work platform, but in a fall can cause serious injuries to the back and other parts of the body. We are, of course, assuming you survive the fall. The proper harness can make the difference.

Next comes the lanyard. This device connects your harness (at the sliding D-ring on the back) to a lifeline or similar anchorage point. It can be no longer than six feet (shorter is okay) and must have a shock absorber. If the lanyard does not have that shock absorber, it isn't OSHA-compliant. Look at it this way; which would you prefer took the shock load if you took a six-foot fall, the shock absorber on the lanyard or your body. Think about it.

In the venues I've visited, most people have the proper harnesses and lanyards. The next part of the system is where I see difficulties begin. The lifeline is a length of cable or rope (either vertical or horizontal depending on the application), which attaches your bad self to the building. It is a critical component of the fall protection system, but I've seen folks use the damnedest things. The most common offenders are ¼" diameter (or smaller) cable with malleable cable clips. I've also seen ⅜" cotton rope. You know, the stuff your grandmother used to hang up the wash. Unrated turnbuckles and rapid links, even S-hooks once. Remember the OSHA requirements about a 5,000 pound tensile strength? S-hooks, cotton rope and unrated equipment don't even come close to meeting that requirement. Most of the manufacturers of fall protection gear make lifelines. Do yourself, your riggers, and your lawyers a favor. Buy a pre-engineered system that is OSHA-compliant from a reputable manufacturer.

Now that lifeline has to be attached to something, right? Can't just hang in midair, can it? Again, when left to their own devices, people tend to make some very odd choices. The lifeline must be attached to the building, lighting truss, whatever in such a manner as to preserve that tensile strength of 5,000 pounds. It's called an anchorage point. Tying the line off to a ⅜" diameter aluminum diagonal truss support member just isn't going to get the job done. Neither is using the seventy-five-year-old wooden pin rail on the fly floor. Remember that discussion about manufactured lifelines? No? (Go ahead, look at the preceding paragraph, we'll wait.) For the most part, the same holds true here. The difference is in who's making the anchorage points. You'll find truss manufacturers along with the fall protection guys involved with this. Makes sense, yes? The majority of lifelines are used on lighting trusses. Somebody has to supply this stuff. And if you are in a place where there is no obvious tie off location, ask! Get an engineer to identify the best location in the facility or, if there are no points, help you design some.

Climbing without the proper equipment is downright silly. If the people you are working for don't provide the equipment and the training, don't climb. It's as simple as that. If you aren't using fall arrest equipment, your chances of becoming a brown spot on the floor with a chalk outline go up quite significantly. C'mon folks. Use your heads.

All too often I get asked, "What should I do if I show up for a rigging call and there aren't any harnesses?" The answer is simple. Don't climb. You can't get fired for refusing to do something illegal. If they do kick you off the job, take them to court. Sue them for a bundle.

Invariably, the next comment is, "But one of the other guys always goes up and it makes me look stupid." Yeah, and becoming a brown spot on the floor with a chalk outline isn't stupid? You have to talk with your peers, your fellow stagehands. Everyone has to learn that there are severe ramifications to ignoring the fall arrest regulations. The possibility of injury or death should be obvious. But if that doesn't work, maybe you could point out that OSHA levies some very hefty fines on employers and employees when infractions are discovered.

Bring a copy of the regulations in to work. The official rules and regulations are available online at www.osha.gov/SLTC/fall-protection/standards.html. Be aware, however, that they are in government speak and may be a bit difficult to digest. There are several good books on the market that can translate them into English. One of my favorites is *Introduction to Fall Protection* by J. Nigel Ellis (3rd edition), published by the American Society of Safety Engineers.

Talk it up at the next union meeting. Or at the softball game. Solidarity is the name of the game here. If you can organize the right response to bad situations – and believe me, not having a fall arrest harness on at 110 feet is a bad situation – then management just may be encouraged to do the right thing. I know I sound like some hippie fresh out of the '60s, but that's okay. After all, it's where I got my start. At least I won't need my tear gas mask and riot helmet for this form of activism. But now I want to move on to the next step.

Rescue

Consider this scenario. A load-in at the local arena goes sour when one of the high steel riggers slips and falls. But happy days! The rigger was using an appropriate fall arrest system and, lo and behold, the equipment worked. Instead of falling seventy-five feet to his death, he's now dangling in a harness eight feet below the I-beam where he was originally working. But the happiness is short lived. Joy is replaced by concern. No one in the building knows how to get him down safely. The personnel lift isn't tall enough. It's 911 time. The police rescue squad arrives soon after, but doesn't have climbing gear on the truck and no high angle rescue training. The fire department is brought in. The truck they bring has a snorkel device long enough to reach the guy, but it's too big to get into the building. They huddle to try and figure out another way. Meanwhile, remember the person who took the fall? He's still dangling up there. And the clock is ticking.

If you take a fall, even the best commercial harness on the market won't protect you from every injury. Muscles get wrenched. You sprain your back. Dangling sixty-seven feet in the air in a fall arrest harness is definitely not a fun thing to do. The sooner you get down, the better off you are. Tests have shown that hanging in a harness longer than twenty minutes seriously increases the risk of death due to harness trauma or other circulatory problems. In short, if you spend too much time hanging in that harness you could die there.

OSHA figured this out also. In addition to the regulations about using the right gear and doing inspections, etc., the OSHA rules go on to say that you have to have a rescue plan in place for each location where a fall arrest system may be needed. Yes. Each and every place. This includes that beam on the other side of the HVAC duct where the LD always insists on hanging a side light truss. These rescue plans must be written down and they must be practiced.

If you stop and think about it for a second, it makes perfect sense. But, unfortunately, we don't take the time to think about it. You know how it goes: get in, get the job done and get out. Move on to the next gig. Coming up with an appropriate rescue plan takes time. And time is money. You only draw a paycheck when you're working, right? And venue owners only make money when the hall is rented, correct? So there is precious little time or incentive to put a plan together. But you must. It is essential that you convince the Powers That Be that putting a rescue plan in place is necessary for the safety of everyone. Watching, helpless, from the floor while a coworker slowly dies in a harness is not a good thing.

Who is responsible for putting this plan together? I'm not going to go into the legal answers because, frankly, that's not my department. My concern is to help keep people alive and safe while they're working. And I believe that means everyone involved in the space is responsible. Certainly the venue owners and managers must be involved. So too should the members of the unions that have jurisdiction there. And yes, the production companies that bring gear and people into the venue. Unless you can guarantee that you will never, ever have an accident in that facility, then you should be involved in the planning and training to handle the situation when you do have one.

You'll be surprised at how easy it can be to formulate a rescue plan. The first step is to determine which emergency department has jurisdiction in the venue. It could be the fire department or the police. If it's a large enough city or if you're in a mountainous region, you might even have a high angle rescue team that you will call. The important thing is to know whom to call before an accident occurs. Remember, that clock is ticking.

The next step is to get a representative from the emergency department together with all of the concerned parties who work in the building to determine where the problem areas are and work out the appropriate rescue responses. Please understand that this will require more than ten minutes of everyone's time and more than the back of an envelope, okay? Take the time to do it right.

It may be that the plans you come up with require the purchase of more safety equipment. Do it. Your staff may require special training. Train them. And then practice. Yes, it's going to take some down time in the venue. Yes, the staff and crew will probably have to donate a Saturday or two. So what? All things considered, it seems a small price to pay.

Once the plan is in place you will need to practice it on a regular basis. The union regularly gets new members who need to be brought up to speed. So do the local production companies. It's also good for the fire department or whoever is responsible from the city. Everyone needs to be reminded what to do from time to time. Hell, I can't remember what I had for breakfast most days. Always keep in mind the reason for all this planning and rehearsal: an accident could happen to anyone on any day. Maybe even to you.

Then there's the issue of record keeping. OSHA is, after all, a government agency and what government agency in its right mind would skip the paperwork? All fall arrest equipment must be inspected and properly maintained, that much by now should be clear. There may come a time when you'll need to prove that you properly inspected and maintained the gear. To do that you'll need a written record, with dates and signatures and everything. (A judge just isn't going to take your word for it, ya know.) Besides, it's really good to know when you bought that harness and how tough a career it's had. You are, after all, betting your life on it.

There's a joke that runs around the rigging community: It's not the fall that kills, but the sudden stop at the bottom. Well, we've come a long way in eliminating that possibility. The planning and the training will pay off, big time; if ever there is a need for them. Just remember. You want to live long enough to be a burden to your children.

Using Personnel Lifts Safely

And now, just as we're gathering up our belongings and getting ready to leave, and I'm thinking about putting my feet up with a nice glass of wine, some smarty pants in the back rows raises his hand and asks about personnel lifts. "Do I need a harness in a Genie?" he asks. The short answer to his question is that every lift manufacturer, be it of a single mast style "Genie" to a fifty-foot tall scissors lift, will identify what, if any, type of fall arrest is required in its lifts. Like it or not, you have to read the manual.

But the problem with personnel lifts is not fall arrest. The real problem is the darn things keep falling over. And why is that? Because people tend to use personnel lifts improperly and expect to get away with it, that's why.

An acquaintance of mine was injured in a personnel lift accident. Seems he was being rolled around with the basket fully raised and him in it. Dumb, dumb and dumber. Why do people insist on being stupid with Genies and other lifts? I think it's because there's a force field around all personnel lifts that lowers the IQ of the people using them by fifty points! Yeah, that's got to be it.

Genies and other personnel lifts are perfectly safe when used correctly. When used incorrectly they are death traps. We all know the rules, but we are going to run through them one more time. Please repeat after me:

- I will not use a Genie or other personnel lift without the supplied outriggers, no matter what.

- I will not move a Genie or other personnel lift while the basket is raised and a person is in the basket, no matter what.

- I will not use a Genie or other personnel lift on uneven ground without first leveling the lift, no matter what.

Okay? Okay. Geez. The things I have to do. Now go outside and play nice with the other kids.

Motorized Rigging

The inspiration for this chapter came from a recent trip to London where I had the opportunity to see three shows. Incurable technician that I am, I couldn't help looking at the tech stuff. Two of the shows used motorized rigging and the third one probably should have. So I'm going to share some thoughts with you about motorized rigging. (This will be a lot more fun if you imagine we're talking over a Newcastle Brown at that pub just down the street from the Gatwick Theatre stage door.)

The most common type of motorized rigging is the cable drum winch. A cable drum winch is a machine that runs on electricity (usually), hydraulics (rarely) or pneumatics (almost never) and moves scenery by winding up or paying out a steel cable. The movement can be vertical, horizontal or a combination of the two.

To get a picture of what a winch looks like, here are the major components: (Sung to the tune of "The shinbone is connected to the thighbone.") The motor is connected to the gearbox and the gearbox is connected to the cable drum. The cable drum is connected to the lift cable and the lift cable is connected to the scenery. (Mitch Miller, eat your heart out.)

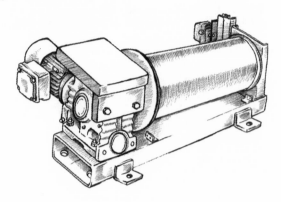

It all starts with the motor. This is a device that takes in electricity and converts that electricity to movement. There is a metal rod, called a shaft that runs through the motor and sticks out one end of the motor. The motor has one job and one job only: to spin the shaft. When the motor is switched on, i.e., electricity is run into it, the shaft starts to spin. Most motors will spin a shaft at about 1,750 revolutions per minute (RPM). The problem with the motor, however, is that it's got no oomph. It goes fast, yes, but it has no strength behind it. Lots of scenery weighs in at well over 1,000 pounds these days and a spinning motor shaft is not going to make a lift by itself. To add strength to the speed of the motor, a transmission is needed.

The transmission, or gear reducer, is essentially a metal housing enclosing a series of toothed gears. The gear reducer takes the speed of the turning motor shaft and converts that speed into power (called "torque" in engineer speak). This is achieved by developing a mechanical advantage. In this case, the different sized gears working together inside the gear reducer create the mechanical advantage. The motor shaft comes into the gear reducer spinning at 1,750 RPM but has no real power to do much of anything, except spin. The gear reducer, with its inherent mechanical advantage, takes that spinning shaft, slows it down and gives it the muscle it needs to lift a heavy weight. How large a weight it can lift is determined by the size (measured in horsepower) of the motor and the amount of mechanical advantage created by the gear reducer.

For example, let's say you want to raise a 1,800 pound lighting pipe and you just happen to have a one horsepower motor lying around. And let's add in a desired speed of about sixteen to twenty feet per minute. The motor, which has a shaft speed of 1,750 RPM, won't be able to lift the pipe by itself, but if you slap a 200:1 gear reducer onto it you can easily lift the pipe. The speed will be right at seventeen feet per minute.

If you want a clearer picture of how this works, pull the transmission out of your car, stick it on a band saw and slice it in half. (Do this outside, though, as it can get a bit messy.) Or if you don't feel like ruining your car, go over to your local pediatrician's office. There's this toy they keep in most waiting rooms I've been in (hey, I've got three kids). It has a bunch of different sized gears that you put together on a pegboard table. When you're done assembling the thing you turn the crank at one end and all the gears turn and then something moves at the other end. It's way cool. (I never get to finish putting it together before the nurse comes. I hate that.)

Manufacturers of gearboxes have specifications for lubrication. Be advised, however, that these specs are written for industrial users, not us theatre folk. Their specs call for replacing the oil after about a zillion hours of use. In an industrial application this may be once a month. In the theatre it could translate to once every ten years. Inaction, as we all should know, can be just as dangerous as action. If you don't use that motor very often the oil begins to turn to sludge at the bottom. Less and less oil gets to the gears when you turn it on. To insure that your gearbox runs smoothly you should check the oil at least once a year. If it looks dirty, or you see stuff swimming around in it, change it.

Now we need to figure out how to connect the motor to the gearbox. One common way is to use a large roller type chain drive. (Think of a bicycle chain on steroids.) First a metal sprocket – a wheel with teeth around the rim – is put onto the motor shaft. Then a sprocket is attached to the shaft that runs into the gearbox. Finally, a loop of roller chain is wrapped around the two sprockets.

Bingo! You're hooked up. Now, in addition to turning the gears in the gearbox, you can also make neat motorcycle noises when you turn the motor on. (For instructions on how to make motorcycle noises without actually having a motor, talk to a kid – any kid. They all know how.)

Another way to connect the motor to the gearbox would be to butt the end of the motor shaft up against the end of the gearbox shaft and connect the two with a device called a shaft coupler. Couplers are okay in certain situations, but it can be difficult to find couplers rated for overhead lifting. And using a coupler means adding more hardware to the system; hardware that requires inspection and maintenance. If I were you I'd avoid using a shaft coupler whenever possible. But if you really have to use one, make sure it's rated for overhead lifting.

The third – and safest – way to get those gears turning is called "direct drive." With this method the shaft coming out of the motor is long enough to run completely through the gearbox. So when the motor turns on, it's the single shaft running through the motor and gearbox that is turning. It's a less complex assembly than the other two methods and there is less hardware involved. Less hardware means there's less opportunity for something to go wrong.

We still have that piece of scenery sitting on the floor waiting patiently to get lifted, right? Not to worry, we're getting closer to a solution.

The cable drum is the last major component that's needed to get the scenery moving. The drum is a length of large diameter pipe that, as it rotates, winds up and pays out the lift cable. It is usually mounted directly to the gearbox output shaft, but is sometimes driven by a roller chain. And sometimes there's a coupler between the drum and gearbox. But, as noted earlier, direct drive is the best (and safest) solution.

One of the important characteristics of a drum is that it has to be grooved. This groove, which is equal to the diameter of the cable that will be used on it, is helically cut into the drum's outer surface. (Think of a tightly wrapped spiral here.) This groove insures that the cable wraps up neatly on the drum when you are lifting or moving the piece of scenery. It's dangerous to use a drum that isn't grooved as the cable can flop around wherever it wants to and it's a safe bet that it will go where you don't want it to go. The cable can cross over on itself, wrap around the shaft or wrap around some other piece of equipment associated with the drum. Any of those scenarios can cause problems ranging from bouncing scenery, to cable damage or failure. (Audiences hate it when the scenery falls down and smacks their favorite actor in the head.) Always use a grooved drum and make sure the groove is the right size for the cable you are using.

Another important requirement is that the drum is long enough to allow all of the cable to wrap on it in a single layer. Cable wrapping over itself on a drum that is too short can cause jams, kinks and even breaks in the cable.

So that's the basic assembly. A motor spinning a shaft connected to a gear reducer that adds torque to the spinning shaft and a drum that has the room to collect the cable. You could do the job with just these three things, but you can't do it safely. To do this kind of thing safely you need a couple more devices.

If you can remember way back when I was talking about the motor, I said there was a shaft sticking out one end of it. Well, I lied. That shaft actually runs through the motor and sticks out both ends. One end goes into the gear reducer and the other end just sort of, well, sticks out. Some bright soul saw the shaft waving in the breeze as an opportunity and stuck a brake on it. This motor brake clamps down on the shaft when the power is turned off. It doesn't matter if the power was shut down on purpose or accidentally. If the shaft doesn't turn, nothing else in the system is going to move either. This is a good thing. Think of it as leaving your car parked on a hill with the transmission in neutral. Without a brake engaged the car will start rolling down the hill. If you happen to be in San Francisco your car will start rolling really fast and, even if you are an Olympic sprinter, you won't catch it.

Occasionally a second brake is added to the system. This one is called an over-speed brake. It's mounted onto the shaft on the opposite end of the cable drum from the gear reducer. Its job is to stop the drum from turning too fast. For example, you are lowering the drawbridge in *Man of La Mancha* and suddenly the bridge starts moving faster than it's supposed to go. Maybe the shaft driving the drum broke or the drive chain between the motor and gear reducer failed. In any event, you don't really have time to go and investigate the problem. What you need to do is stop the bridge from moving now, before someone gets hurt. The over-speed brake is designed to sense that increase in speed and will stop the drum by clamping down on the shaft. This is why it's put on the opposite end of the winch system. No matter what fails in between the drum and the motor, the over-speed brake will still stop the drum.

And last but certainly not least, we have the control system. How you make the winch do what you want is key to a successful cue. There are elebenty-seven different types of control systems on the market today and a zillion variations on each one of them. What kind of system you get depends on your needs and your budget. For today we're gonna keep it simple.

You got your up, down and emergency stop buttons. Simple enough, eh? The up and down buttons are momentary ones. What we call a "deadman's" (deadwoman's?) switch. You have to hold the button down for the unit to operate. If you get tired or bored, if you fall asleep or pass out and your finger comes off the button, the unit stops. The emergency stop (E-stop) button is there for the inevitable emergency. It's usually something like the up or down button getting stuck (that's what happens when soda gets spilled on them). The E-stop is called a mushroom head because that's what it looks like. Not a portabello or anything. Just your regular old garden-variety mushroom. To engage it all you have to do is smack it. You should be able to hit it even during an earthquake.

The ability to add more complicated equipment – master switches, indicator lights, computer control, etc. – is directly proportional to the depth of your pockets. Go ahead and buy what you want and can afford. But, always, always, always get a manual override to go along with the cutesy stuff. You will need it. No control system is infallible. Eventually you will be sitting there with a system that doesn't work with show time in a half hour. You will want to kiss the manual override at that point.

So now you can run the winch up and down and you can stop it by letting go of the button. But how about those times when you need to repeat a cue, something like a backdrop coming in to position, several times during a performance? You can't rely on pulling your finger off the button at the exact right moment every night, right? This is where limit switches come in very handy.

Limit switches are electromechanical devices that, when engaged, stop the winch from moving by turning off a control circuit. There are several different types of switches used in the entertainment business but the most common is the four-pole rotary limit switch. This is a device that has four gears mounted on a shaft. Each gear has a specific function. There's one to stop the unit when it's going up and one to stop it when it's going down. The other two limits switches are safety switches, usually called the ultimate limit switches. One works for the up operation and the other works for the down operation. (Or in/out if the action calls for horizontal movement.)

Engaging an ultimate limit switch will shut down the winch. You will then have to go and find the problem, fix it and then reset the limit before the winch will run again. The limit switch is engaged by means of a cam on each gear. This cam is a small nub protruding out from the rim of the gear. When the gear rotates the cam swings around and hits a button. That's the switch.

What makes the limit switch gears rotate is the really important part. It's all about more gears, shafts and chains. (Once engineers find something they like it's hard for them to let go, ya know?)

The limit switches live in a small squarish box mounted to the winch frame. The limit switch drive shaft, which sticks out of the box, has a sprocket on it. The shaft sticking out of the cable drum also has a sprocket on it. A roller chain wraps around the two sprockets, connecting them in a closed loop. When one shaft turns so does the other. You now you have positive communication between the drum and the limit switches. Without this communication between the drum shaft and the limit switch shaft, the limit switch shaft simply wouldn't work. This makes that limit switch drive shaft roller chain really, really important.

While reading all this you're probably thinking that there's a lot of equipment involved here and something could go wrong. And you would be right. The more pieces the better the chances for something to fail. All the shafts and sprockets have set screws and roll pins holding them in place. Without proper maintenance set screws loosen and fall out. The itty-bitty connectors that join the ends of the chain together can also work loose over time. If any one of these devices fails then communication between the cable drum and the limit switch is lost. The limit switch then has no idea when to tell the winch to stop. You can imagine what would happen if a 2,000 pound piece of scenery being lowered at thirty-five feet per minute wasn't told to stop when it reached the stage floor. Ouch.

The best way to avoid scenarios like the one above is to follow a stringent inspection and maintenance schedule. If you check the machine for wear or problems on a regular basis then chances are you won't have any exciting (albeit gory) stories to tell about your motorized rigging system.

1. Check oil levels in the gearbox.
2. Change gearbox oil at least every two
   years - more often if it looks dirty.
3. Make sure the drive chains and the limit switch
   chains have all their parts and are lubricated properly.
4. Tighten all those set screws, bolts and nuts regularly.
5. Have the unit professionally maintained once a year.

So the moral of the story is this. Ignorance is not bliss. Ignoring your equipment will only lead to disaster. And disasters always cut into your personal time. Make sure your winches get all the attention they require and you'll have time to finish that rousing game of Monopoly in the green room.

-6-
Staying Safe

What is it about the holiday season that causes normal people to lose their minds? Beginning in late October I start getting calls from community group technical directors, church deacons and high school music teachers who want to fly an actor in their holiday shows. Invariably, the first thing out of their mouths, after they tell me what they want to do, is "but we don't have much money so it has to be cheap." These are intelligent, responsible people. People, who probably pay their taxes on time, get regular dental check-ups and wear their seat belts even when driving just two blocks. What on earth would lead these fine upstanding citizens to believe that suspending their children from little ropes and wires over a stage for cheap is a good idea?

"We're only going to be lifting her six feet in the air," they say. "Fine," I respond. "Why don't you stand on top of a six-foot stepladder, jump off and land on the base of your spine to see what it feels like. Then tell me if you want your kid in that position." Sometimes that gets their attention.

I hear it all. They want no supervision. They want me to sell them some rope, a pulley and a cheap harness and turn them loose on the Peter Pans and flying angels of the world. I have the same answer for each and every one of them. "No."

People think that just anything tied around a person will work as a flying harness. They trot off to Home Depot looking for a safety harness. The ever-knowledgeable salesperson (at Home Depot?) simply stares at them of course, not having a clue. That's when they call me. When I explain that all I carry are fall arrest or climbing harnesses, they ask if they can alter one of those. I tell them no and explain why these harnesses will not work; the harnesses aren't designed for this type of stunt nor do the manufacturers warrant their use in this manner. Then I recommend that they talk to one of the companies that make flying harnesses. "Those people are too expensive," I'm told. Oh. What do you think that six-foot fall is going to do to your kid's spine? Is it worth putting the kid in a wheelchair for life because you were too cheap to get the right harness? Some of the parents even listen at this point. For the others I move onto my next argument.

Experience. There's a difference between the volunteer, who runs the fly rail once a year at the church pageant, and the professional who's been running a fly system for years. The difference, among other things, is focus. Let's look at a possible scenario. Poindexter, the volunteer, is running the rail. He is seventeen and a senior in high school. He has a girlfriend, and she just walked backstage to chat during a rehearsal. Is this kid giving his total attention to the show or is he showing off for his girlfriend? Go ahead; think back to when you were seventeen. He's even more easily distracted because he's in unfamiliar surroundings and he doesn't really understand the repercussions of a mistake. And then there's Amy, the professional, who does know what happens to someone who is dropped from six feet or run into a wall. She also knows that she can wait and take her boyfriend out for donuts after the rehearsal.

The professional also knows when to call it quits. When a flying effect works, amateur directors tend to act like they invented it all by themselves. They want to do it everywhere and all the time. Flying is an extremely tiring undertaking, both for the performer and the technician. You've got to know when to draw the line and stop working before someone gets hurt. It's also smart to understand that not everyone in the cast has to fly. Cap'n Hook, played by somebody's paunchy dad, never looks good careening around on a wire. Eventually I get through to most of these folks and they either call in a professional or don't do the gag. But I'm willing to bet there are plenty of others who don't bother to call and are blithely flinging their kids around a stagehouse. If you happen to know any folks like that let them know just how foolish their actions are and try to get them to stop. It'll be your good deed for the week.

Maintenance and Inspections

Flying people around the stage is all well and good, and it's even fun. But it's not something we do very often. What we do often is fly scenery and lights and sound equipment. To do that we need rigging stuff. Lots of it. And that stuff (machinery, actually) needs attention. You wouldn't drive your car around for years on end without a mechanic having an occasional look under the hood, right? The same holds true for your rigging equipment. To keep your gear running well you need to pay attention to it.

It has always amazed me that even in the big-time universities and arts centers there is almost never a documented (read: written down on a piece of paper that is then put in a place where someone can find it later) maintenance program. Occasionally, a production assistant might get sent up to the grid to "look around" but if he/she doesn't record what he/she did, no one remembers it the next day.

All rigging systems require maintenance. I don't care if it's a single dead-hung pipe or a forty-motor grid system; parts is parts and they need to be checked. The first step is to consult the owner's manual that came with the system. You say you never got a manual? Lost the one you had, Bunky? Well, use Mr. Bell's handy-dandy invention. Call the supplier. Call the dealer. Call the manufacturer. Insist that they send you owner's manuals. The manual should not only tell you how to operate the system, but also identify all of the major components of that system and their respective maintenance schedules. If the manual does not have this information, call the supplier, call the dealer, etc. (see above).

Once you have the manual and all the necessary information to maintain your system, *do it.* And when you do it, *write it down.* Record it in a logbook and put the book in a safe place. (That means someplace where coffee won't get spilled on it, someplace where it can't be mistaken for a drop cloth, someplace where stray animals won't be tempted to eat it.) Then refer to it often. Let your friends read it. And when the inspector comes, let him/her read it, too. It's kind of a sharing thing.

Which brings us, and rather adroitly I thought, to safety inspections. How to cover your butt, sleep at night, and not get your hands too dirty.

A safety inspection should cover all aspects of the performance area. Fire and electrical safety systems, rigging systems and the equipment hung from them should all be inspected, along with operating procedures and general housekeeping. This is where that maintenance logbook comes in. The inspector(s) get to read this, learn a little about your facility, and review your maintenance practices. If you're smart, you'll send them copies of the log in advance of the actual inspection. That way they will be better prepared to do your inspection, and you'll get a more complete and efficient job.

If you only read one line of this section, make it the following: *Have your facility inspected once a year.* Period. No ifs, ands or buts. If the place gets used on a regular basis, inspect it on a regular basis. Stage rigging involves machinery. The various components of the system move and, because of that movement, the parts of the system will eventually wear out. That is the primary reason for having your stage rigging inspected. If that's not motivation enough, there are several other reasons for an annual safety inspection. The people using the equipment may not know how to operate it properly, and therefore may cause damage to some of the parts. The equipment may not have been installed properly or – and this happens more often that you'd think – the wrong equipment may have been installed in the first place.

You can imagine the damage that a thirty-pound lighting instrument will do when it falls from forty-five feet up, or when the entire back wall of a set breaks away from the pipe batten and crashes to the floor. People call these incidents "accidents" but that's not entirely accurate. These incidents are caused by neglect. When a rope or cable or other piece of hardware breaks, it doesn't usually do so without warning. The component may twist or stretch long before it fails. A good rigging inspector will discover this problem and advise you as to how to prevent these potential "accidents."

By way of example, let's look at one element in a counter-weight system; the operating line. This line is used to raise and lower the pipe batten (and consequently, whatever is attached to that pipe) over the stage. The rope is made of manila or, in a newer theatre, a synthetic rope (usually polyester). The current industry standard mandates that manila rope should be replaced about every seven years. The synthetic ropes last two to three times longer. But these are just guidelines and many things can affect the lifespan of a rope. An inspector will check the ropes for wear, abrasion points, abrupt changes in the size or shape of the rope and in the case of manila, dry rot. He or she will be able to tell you if the rope needs replacing now or at some point in the near future. Remember, if that rope breaks something will fall, either the pipe batten or the counter-weight arbor. Either way, someone could get seriously hurt.

Hire an outside organization to do the inspection. I don't recommend doing in-house inspections, as you would incur a considerable amount of liability. There are a number of firms in the United States that offer rigging inspections as part of their services. Choosing one need not be a painful task. The theatre business is a very small industry and the number of companies offering inspections in this country is even smaller. Start your search with your local theatrical supplier who can probably refer a rigging inspector to you. If that doesn't work, and you are a member of a theatre organization, ask someone there. Failing that, there is always the Internet. Two organizations with sites that may help are USITT (United Institute for Theatre Technology, www.usitt.org) and ESTA (Entertainment Services and Technology Association, www.esta.org).

Once you have identified several companies to talk with, here are some questions to ask to help you pick the right one for your facility:

1. Request a formal proposal. This proposal should outline the costs for the project and tell you what services will be included. You want to make sure that the company will not only inspect the stage rigging, but also the equipment hanging from the rigging. The inspector should also check out other areas where you may have equipment; for example, lighting positions over the seating area on pipes or catwalks. You want someone who is ready and willing to climb over every inch of the place, going where no one has gone before, dragging weird testing tools. The quality and clarity of the proposal is also a good indication of what the written report will look like.

2. Find out how long it will take to get the written report after the inspection is complete. Also find out what kind of information the report will give you. Will it identify the problems found? Will the report also offer solutions to those problems and give you a cost estimate for those repairs?

3. Get references and check them.

Because theatres come in all shapes and sizes, it's difficult to tell how long the inspection will actually take. For a typical high school theatre you should expect the inspection to take four to six hours. A larger theatre, with more complicated equipment, will take longer. (The Filene Center for the Performing Arts at Wolftrap in Washington, D.C., takes three days!)

The costs for a rigging inspection vary from company to company but normally range from about 700 to 1,500 dollars. You might also be expected to cover travel costs, which could include airfare, a hotel room and meals, depending on where the inspector is based.

Whatever you do, please don't ignore your stage equipment. Have your stage rigging inspected regularly. As stagehands are fond of saying, "Gravity still works but it's not always your friend."

Fire Curtains

While we're on the subject of maintenance and inspections, let's take a stroll over to what is probably the least understood part of a stage rigging system, but may be its most important part. I'm referring, of course, to fire curtains.

Before I start, however, I want to throw in a disclaimer. As of this writing both ESTA and NFPA (National Fire Protection Association) have been working furiously (but separately) on fire curtain standards, but as neither organization has finalized its work yet I cannot reference them here. However, by the time you are reading this it is likely that one or both organizations will have published a standard, so you might want to check their websites. Regardless of when these standards are adopted however, this section is written for those of you who already have fire curtains.

Question: What do you have if there is a fire onstage, the overhead smoke doors open and the fire curtain does *not* operate properly. *Answer*: A kiln. (This is not a good thing.)

In the good old days a fire curtain was made of asbestos. In fact, in many municipalities you had to have the word ASBESTOS written clearly in really big letters on the front of the curtain. You also had to show it to the audience before every performance. If you did that these days your audience would, of course, be out the door before you could say "carcinogenic." Since the mid-1970s, fire curtains have been made of materials other than asbestos, usually a silica based material.

Why do we have a fire curtain? (I mean, other than another way for rigging companies to make money?) There are a number of reasons. Here are two:

To a fire, a proscenium opening is nothing more than a big hole in the wall. The fire needs oxygen and combustibles to survive, so it's the fire's desire to jump through that hole to see what it can eat on the other side. The fire curtain is supposed to help stop that from happening.

Another reason is so that your great-aunt Matilda doesn't panic when she sees the set of her favorite show go up in flames. You see, if she does panic, she might faint. If she faints she may block an aisle. If there are fifty great-aunt Matildas in the audience that day, well, you get the picture.

So we have the what and the why (in abbreviated form). What comes next is how.

There are two basic kinds of fire curtains, the straight lift curtain and the brail curtain. A straight lift curtain is hung like a backdrop – suspended from the top. This type of curtain, which must be tall enough to cover the proscenium opening completely, is used when you have enough height above the proscenium arch to lift the curtain out of sight. For example; if your proscenium is sixteen feet high and your stage roof is forty feet, you can lift the curtain straight up and have it disappear.

A brail type curtain is used when there is not enough height above the proscenium to get a straight lift curtain out of sight. A sixteen-foot high proscenium opening and a twenty-eight-foot high stage roof would be an example. With a brail curtain you hang the top of the curtain from the overhead supports and attach the lifting cables to the bottom of the curtain. When you raise the curtain it will pile up on itself. It makes for a rather larger bunch of fabric just above the proscenium, but it's better than no fire curtain at all, right?

Rigging is required for both curtain styles. The straight lift curtain can be operated by a counterweight system, an electric winch or some combination of the two. The brail curtain uses a manually operated hydraulic winch. The winch regulates the descent speed of the curtain. What most of the rigging systems have in common is how they are activated/used/tripped.

It's pretty clear how a fire curtain can be activated when someone is in the theatre at the time of a fire. You smell smoke, you see the fire, you go over and pull on the fire curtain rope or push a button and the fire curtain comes down. Simple. But what about when no one is there, like in the middle of the night when only those pesky gremlins are running about?

The automatic fire release line is your first line of defense. This is a line that is rigged along the upstage side of the proscenium wall. It runs up one side of the proscenium opening, across the stage and down the other side. Along the length of the line is a series of fusible links. These links are an integral part of the line. They are designed to burn through (separate) when the ambient temperature reaches about 160°F (71°C). The fire release line is normally connected to the operating line of the fire curtain rigging, or to the clutch in a motorized system. The line is in tension and that tension is what keeps the mechanism from operating. Once tension is released in the fire release line – you've seen the printed signs "In Case of Fire Cut This Line" – the curtain can descend to the stage floor and seal the proscenium opening.

Tension is created in the fire release line by leaving the counterweight system just a little out of balance. The weight of the fire curtain and its related rigging hardware should be a little more (about fifty pounds or so) than the weight in the counterweight arbor.

When a fire starts onstage, the area backstage gets hot quickly. When it reaches 160°F, one of the fusible links separates, causing the fire release line to come apart. This activates the rigging system and allows the counterweight arbor to rise up, bringing the fire curtain down. It's a basic no frills, bells or whistles type of system.

In many states an electronic release system is also required to be in line with the release line. The fusible links aren't enough. This is where the bells and whistles come in. The electronic system usually has a sensor-activated electro-magnetic switch. The switch holds the release line in tension and if the sensor is activated, the switch is released, releasing the fire release line and thereby releasing the curtain to do its thing. (Lots of releases there, eh?) The sensors are usually of the smoke detector type or the type that measure the rate of heat increase.

One of the problems with a fire release line is that it tends to stretch over time. When it stretches, the fire curtain tends to creep down and, eventually, come into view. When that happens, you have to go back to the release line and adjust it. Another problem is that the fusible links aren't the strongest li'l critters in the world. Over time they may break. Then the curtain comes down. (This is considered a bad thing during the death scene in *Exit the King*.) One of the most common mistakes made to alleviate this problem is to chain the bottom of the counterweight arbor off to the building steel. Go ahead and look. It's probably been done in your theatre. What this means, folks, is that when the line is tripped for real, as in a real fire, the curtain won't move. This is a bad thing. (Remember that kiln part?)

The links need preventive maintenance. Replace them every two years. Several rigging manufacturers make devices that help prevent accidental fire curtain activation. You should check into them. If your fire curtain does not operate properly, you not only risk serious damage to your facility, but also injury, or worse, to anyone who might be onstage or in the house at the time. Here are some rules:

1. Don't disable your fire curtain rigging.
2. Test your fire curtain at least once a month.
3. Have your fire curtain system professionally inspected once a year.

The money spent on maintenance and inspection of your fire curtain and its rigging is a pittance compared to the cost of a fire.

-7-

Taking the Show on the Road

Let's face it. A lot of us have a little gypsy in our blood. We like to move around from time to time. Working in the same place for long periods doesn't always feel quite right. It's hard to explain, I know, but the travel bug is there. So we take shows on the road. It's great fun, but touring also presents some safety issues. Especially when working with outdoor stages. As you can imagine, the outdoors is rife with its own unique set of challenges.

Summer is the time for outdoor events. Until the engineers invent something useful like a skyhook, you'll be looking to hang those lights and speakers from something. That something will most likely be a ground support system of one form or another. A ground support system is a temporary vertical support structure (scaffolding, Genie or Super Lift, etc.) that uses terra firma as the base to support your lighting and speaker rigs, scenery and anything else you may need for your show. (Trees do not count as ground support.) The most obvious examples of ground support systems are the large stadium rock show tours. That monster set that the Rolling Stones toured with? That was a ground support system.

But more prevalent than tours using gigunda systems are the small, community-based festivals that use small stages and limited ground support systems. There have been a number of incidents over the years involving these systems, particularly in high winds and bad weather. One of the more notable accidents being a lighting truss that was knocked over onto Curtis Mayfield in Brooklyn, New York, a few years back when a squall came up too quickly for anyone to respond. By employing a few common sense steps, you can avoid problems with your outdoor rig, no matter what type it may be.

First, make sure the rig is on a firm, level foundation. Materials that do not make for solid foundations are cinder blocks, a pile of 2 x 4s stacked four feet high, or a half dozen VW wheels (*sans* the tires) piled on top of each other. If your rig isn't level, a strong wind can cause the weight of the rig to shift. Once that weight shifts, then the 2 x 4s or wheels or whatever go skittering away.

If you're on uneven ground, either dig up the ground to make it level, or build (as in construct) a foundation. The foundation, be it a wooden structure or concrete pad, must be capable of holding the intended loads. It must also be large enough for the vertical member to sit on and be properly bolted down. For example, if your vertical support is a 12" x 12" tower, the box it sits on should be at least 36" square. If you are using a lifting device like a Genie or a Super Lift, then the box should be as big as the device, including the outriggers.

You should also stabilize the load. If you have a couple thousand pounds worth of video wall or other wind-catching device floating below the truss and a heavy wind comes up, you'll have trouble. That much weight swaying on your rig will tip the balance and may cause a catastrophe. Trust me, you don't want that. Tie down that video wall.

Second, use the outriggers. You know those legs the manufacturer provided with the system that you left in your brother-in-law's U-Store-It shed last winter? Call him up and tell him to load up the pickup and get his butt on over to you. Those outriggers are a very necessary part of your defense against bad weather.

After you have the outriggers in place (and you've given your brother-in-law a beer for his trouble) make sure the horizontal system (the truss) is tied securely to the vertical system. More common sense, yes? You'd be surprised. (Are you sensing a pattern here?) I hate to break it to you, but gaffer's tape and tie line do not a secure connection make. You need to use load-rated hardware and apply it according to the manufacturer's specifications. In the case of the 12" box tower, the tower manufacturer makes a corner block that will allow you to attach the tower to the truss. It's a secure connection that is safe and easy to bolt up. So use it already! In case you're using a Genie or Super Lift, then you have the forks of the lift to deal with. The most common method is to secure a sling around the truss and the lift. Make sure, however, that you attach to the vertical (mast) part of the lift. If you simply wrap around the forks, the sling will slide right off.

And finally, how about some diagonal bracing? Most of us call them guy wires, although I have no idea who Guy is. Take some cable or synthetic rope from the top of the rig (or as near the top as you can) and string the lines down to the ground at a forty-five degree angle. Do this in as many directions (at least three) as possible for each tower. Then anchor those lines to something very large and very heavy. A car door handle, for example, is a bad place to tie off. It's not strong enough. Tying off to an oak tree might work. If it's healthy. Do you know what's going on inside the tree? Tent stakes are commonly used but I sometimes wonder if it's wise to use a little piece of wood driven into the mud to hold up a 4,000 pound lighting rig. Ballast is what you really need. Ballast is something you can measure. Many places use water barrels as ballast. You know how much water can go into each barrel and you know how much water weighs. With the help of a structural engineer you can determine how many barrels you will need. Just don't forget to tie them securely to the rig.

In New York City we don't always have water available. Running a hose from the nearby deli to fill up a dozen fifty-five-gallon water barrels is usually frowned upon by the owner of the deli. And we don't tie off to cars because someone might steal the car and drive off with the rig dragging behind it. A funny sight it may be, but it plays havoc with a production schedule. We use what are called Mafia blocks. These babies are three-foot-square cement blocks that weigh about 2,000 pounds apiece. They even have a tie-off point cast right into the top. Get a forklift to place them where you need them and you're in business. I'll leave the reasoning behind the name choice to your imagination.

So, if you're putting up an outdoor rig, take these steps to protect the people in the area and your rig. And don't forget to check the weather reports. Have a good summer.

Market Week

Speaking of summer, August in New York City can be dreadful. It's hot and humid and the air hangs there like curtains in an old age home. Work-wise, there's not much going on. Fortunately, September brings relief. The air turns crisp and the leaves start to do their thing. The Big Apple begins to return to what passes for normal. And, oh joy, oh rapture, work picks up. In addition to a new season on Broadway there are new shows off-Broadway and off-off-Broadway (wherever that is). There's usually a new round of street events requiring tech support and, of course, there's Market Week. Market Week is a week long extravaganza featuring American clothing designers in all their, ahem, glory. Runways spring up all over town and you can't swing a feather boa without hitting at least one supermodel. It is, to say the least, bedlam in Gotham.

Trying to respond to the needs of these somewhat eccentric clients can be a little trying. I thought you might like to get a glimpse into how these shows get put together. Besides, I'm tired of writing about stuff falling down.

I should start with a little history. Prior to 1993 any fashion designer who wanted to do a show simply pulled the display racks out of his or her showroom in midtown, set up a runway, hung lights from the ceiling and invited friends, relations and the press to come to the show. What you ended up with was 250 guests, two dozen models, a zillion lights (all running at full) and a runway all crammed into a twenty-foot by eighty-foot space. And let's not forget the forty or so photographers crammed onto the press platform. It was a fire marshal's worst nightmare.

Multiply this scenario by thirty or so designers and you have the earliest, and ugliest, version of Market Week. Not only were the glitterati scurrying around town trying to catch the latest from Calvin Klein, Nicole Miller and the like, but the technicians too were racing back and forth making sure that the right gear went to the right site at the right time. It was nuts.

Then in 1993, Mike Sapsis, who was, and still is by the way, my identical twin brother, cooked up a scheme with the folks at the New York Public Library (NYPL). He wanted to do fashion shows in rep.

The NYPL has a space on the first floor called the Celeste Bartos Forum that is perfect for this sort of event. It's large enough to hold 250 people legally and small enough to make the shows intimate. The idea was to set up a runway and stage, hang a basic lighting plot and then let the designers come in and add what they wanted.

We ran, on average, about four shows a day. Now, instead of running all over midtown lugging gear from showroom to showroom, we could stay put and let the designers (and the models) come to us. We were in tech heaven.

Each designer brought in an LD to develop specials that would help make the show look unique. There was the inevitable wailing and gnashing of teeth as the price for these extras was haggled over, but eventually the design was finalized. We supplied the board op and lighting crew. It worked well for several seasons. It was happening. So happening, in fact, that it wasn't long before the Forum was no longer large enough for all the designers who wanted to show. That's when the Council of Fashion Designers of America (CFDA) stepped in. To accommodate the added shows, the CFDA set up a tent next door in Bryant Park. Now we had the Forum and the tent and life was good.

The good life didn't last long. The library did a renovation and access to the Celeste Bartos Forum was severely limited. Bringing a show into the space became very difficult so the venue was no longer used. To compensate, the CFDA, along with the ubiquitous corporate sponsor, brought in bigger tents. In the larger tents were now three separate venues.

Which brings us to the present. These tents are clear span so there are no tent poles to block the audience's view (of each other). The clear span, however, does make for some interesting rigging situations. The tents tend to be different from year to year. When it's a tent that hasn't been used before, getting accurate load ratings can sometimes be a challenge. There's no guessing when it comes to loads in a tent. A lighting rig, complete with hoists, trusses and cable, can be a significant load and it just wouldn't do to have it come down in the middle of a show. (Or anytime, for that matter.) Once we determine the load ratings, the next step is to design the brackets that will attach to the tent structure and allow for the suspension of all the gear needed for the show.

Load-in day can also be interesting. This is New York City remember. Bryant Park is at 40th Street and Sixth Avenue and there's nothing so capricious as New York City traffic. Load-ins usually start early on Sunday morning. You would expect little or no traffic, right? Sometimes yes and sometimes no. I've seen the Lincoln Tunnel backed up to the Jersey Turnpike, which is a very discouraging sight. And once there was a block party on Ninth Avenue and it was closed for the day. The detour made the four cross-town blocks of 40th Street to Bryant Park nothing but taxicabs as far as the eye could see.

When you do get to the site, you find one, and only one, entrance for your gear. (The folks who designed Bryant Park didn't envision fashion shows. They were thinking more like benches, green grass and pigeons.) And all the vendors are trying to get their trucks unloaded at the same time. The rent for the park, you see, can't be cheap and the tents don't go up any sooner than they have to. That means that everybody; lighting, sound, audio, video – even the port-a-potty guys – are all loading in at the same time. It's maybe a little crazy sometimes, what with the fork lifts running back and forth, radios on everyone's hips blaring out commands – "Hey Joe, when you go to the corner get me a coffee will ya?" – but it's fun. Most of the companies involved have been here before and know what to expect. So it goes pretty smoothly. You even get help from some of the other guys when you rip a castor off one of your road boxes. (Of course it's the one full of steel cable.)

Inside the tents it's choreographed mayhem. Everyone has a job to do and everyone needs to be in the same place at the same time. Wear your deodorant and a smile cause your new best buddy is an electrician who's reaching over your right shoulder to hang lights on the truss that you haven't got off the floor yet.

In ten hours the main rigs are in along with the runways and scenery. Focus calls run though the night. In the morning the rehearsals begin. That's when the models show up. But of course you aren't there. You went back to the hotel to get some sleep, remember? And you don't have to be back to the tent for a week when it's time to strike everything. By then the models are on their way to Paris, or Milan or some other exotic location. And you're back in Bryant Park with the port-a-potties

What? And give up show business?

Uncle Bill Hits the Road

I must have been out of my mind. I certainly had no business being there or doing what I was attempting. The there was Houston, Texas. What I was doing was driving an 800-pound Harley Davidson Ultra Classic Electra Glide motorcycle at sixty-five miles per hour through the rain on I-10. On &$##*!@ grooved pavement. And it looked like I was gonna die.

Turn the clock back one year. A couple of us were sitting in my booth at the USITT conference in Minneapolis in 2003 whining because the next USITT was going to be in Long Beach,

California. We were trying to find a way to make the trip a little fun, or at least bearable.

One of us suggested that maybe we could ride motorcycles cross-country to the conference. Then we could use the bikes in the booth. This had a certain appeal to me in a mid-life crisis sort of way. Never mind that I hadn't been on a motorcycle for any serious amount of time in over twenty-five years. Here was my chance to do a Dennis Hopper imitation (a long time dream) and save money on booth furniture. We sat around fantasizing about driving through the countryside until Eric suggested, "Well, gee, maybe you could do it as a fund raiser." That turned the fantasy into a reality and the Long Beach Long Riders were born.

What had started out as bravado over beers now needed to get organized. We had the name, now we needed a team. We talked to friends and we sent out some feelers over the Internet. In short order we had our group put together. The team consisted of eight bikes, one passenger, two chase car drivers, a graphics/website person and a representative from the organization the ride was benefiting – Broadway Cares/Equity Fights AIDS. Next came the organizing part.

Ever heard the phrase "herding cats"? Sometimes, after an evening of discussing the merits of heated vests ad nauseam, that's what it seemed like. But, nine months and over 1,700 emails after we started, we had pulled it together. There were now thirteen brave souls, most of whom barely knew each other, who had worked very hard to put the trip together. We represented eight states and two Canadian provinces and we were as ready as we were gonna be. For what, we weren't sure, but we were ready.

The snow was a little disconcerting. Greg's house in Boone, North Carolina, had been designated as the starting point. Greg's house, mind you is 4,200 feet up on the side of a mountain. Two days before our arrival had seen a six-inch snowfall. I wasn't sure how the hell I was going to get down the driveway, let alone cover the 2,500 miles to Long Beach. The damn thing looked like a ski jump. With a lot of hard work on Greg and Alice's part, and a turbo space heater mounted on a dolly, the driveway was clear and dry on departure day. I remember someone saying that all we had to do was make it down the mountain and we were home free.

But make it down the mountain we did. Out of the snow clouds and into the sunshine. Yeeeeha! C'mon California! The adventure had begun.

The first two days saw us rumbling through the southeast to Baton Rouge. The weather was great. (Those heated vests had been turned off three hours into the ride, never to be turned on again.) The group started to get comfortable with each other's riding styles. Mornings were spent, coffee mugs in hand, standing around the bikes discussing the merits of one piece of equipment over another. (We were, after all, a bunch of backstage gearheads.) Dinner was all about getting to know each other. The trip was happening. So much effort had gone into putting this together, from plotting the route to booking hotel rooms to fund-raising, that it was almost surreal to actually be on the road.

You know how you sometimes get the sense that maybe things are going too well? That looking-over-the-shoulder feeling that something is about to happen. Yeah, well, in my case that something was Texas. Texas was lots and lots of rain. How I survived I-10 in Houston is beyond me. Somehow I missed the Chevy van and regained control of the bike, almost soiling my knickers in the process. But I'd lost my nerve and the rain was my nemesis for the next day-and-a-half. I wanted to drive slower and told the rest of the gang to go on, that I would catch up. They wouldn't hear of it and rallied around me, "We started as a group," Moe said, "and we'll ride as a group. If you want to go slower, we'll all go slower." And that's how we rode till the rain stopped the next day.

By this time we were fast friends. At first I was surprised at how well we all got along, considering most of us were strangers up until three days ago. But it made sense when I remembered what we all had in common. We all shared a love of motorcycles and we all worked backstage.

And so the ride continued. A thunderstorm west of San Antonio had us under an overpass for a while. (Do you know how hard it is to find a bridge in west Texas? This one appeared with only minutes to spare.) A lunch stop in Ozona, Texas, gave the local population something to talk about for a while. The place was called The Café Next Door and they served a great fried chicken lunch. With our group in there along with the after church crowd (it was Sunday) the place was more than a little crowded. But everyone had a good time. Alice even got a donation to the cause from the owners.

After that it was the west Texas desert. Miles and miles of brown dirt and tumbleweeds. And big trucks. Truck drivers tend to be bike riders so they looked out for us. Four of us had CB radios and the truckers would let us know what to expect down the road. In one of the more bizarre small world instances I've seen, as we passed a semi near Yuma, Arizona, Wayne discovered that he knew the driver. They'd been neighbors back east for a while. Hadn't seen the guy in years. They caught up on each other's news at eighty-five miles an hour on I-8.

Banvard got into a CB discussion with one of the truckers about the ride and the charity aspect of it. The trucker wasn't all that sure he approved of an AIDS benefit ride, but Michael persisted. I think he may have made a convert in the end. Or he may have just worn him down.

And that's pretty much how the rest of the trip went. No accidents. No one got hurt and there were no major mechanical problems. Greg did have his throttle cable break east of El Paso, but we cobbled something together with some gaff tape and a pair of needle nose vise grips and he made it to the Harley shop for repairs.

Six days out of Boone, North Carolina, we pulled up to the front doors of the Hyatt in Long Beach. Richard Pilbrow and his wife Molly were just checking in to the hotel as we dismounted. Needless to say, they got drafted into service as the "official greeters" and were pulled into the group photos.

The conference was a blur of events and meetings. One of the high points for me was the raffle we ran on Saturday. Don't know exactly how much money we raised with it but it was good fun. And speaking of money, a zillion thanks to our many friends who donated time, money or services.

I've had defining moments in my life but I've always had to look back to see them and recognize them for what they were. This time I was smack in the middle of it when I realized what this experience was going to mean to me. Maybe it was, as Moe had said, that we started out as a group and finished as one. Or maybe it was because we all looked out for each other all the time, on the road and off. It could have been the peals of laughter coming from the dinner table night after night or the strangely comforting sight of seeing Cris working on his bike every morning before breakfast. It was all of that and so much more.

Thank you Greg, Alice, Mike, Wayne, Moe, Cris, Pat, Loren, John, Rob, Sarah and Joe. Thank you for sharing this adventure with me. Please know that I will ride with you anytime and anywhere.

And for the rest of you bikers out there, this was our inaugural ride, not our only one. No way were we going to let this be a one-time thing. As of this writing, we're planning our third ride. The second ride, in 2005, was an even bigger success than the first. We raised over $28,000 and had a blast. The ride has become an annual event.

A number of my *HEADS!* newsletter readers have asked what it's like to work in other countries. I've been extremely lucky in my career in that I get to spend a fair amount of time overseas, be it for a show or teaching a class. Like many well-traveled people I know, I can't stop yakking about the places I've been and the people I've met. It's one of the very cool things about my job. But you do need to be careful. If you show an interest in listening to me, I may have to bring out the PowerPoint presentation.

As you know, it can get hot onstage. During a summer rigging installation, we had the loading dock doors wide open, hoping for a little breeze. I was up on the grid when I heard bells. You know, the tinkling sounds of my childhood – the neighborhood ice cream truck! With a whoop and a holler I ran for the door, calling for the crew to follow. Reality sunk in as I left the building and saw the truck. I wasn't anywhere near my neighborhood. I was, in fact, in Taipei, Taiwan. And in Taipei, as in many other places, those bells do not signify the arrival of an ice cream truck. It's the trash truck. (That little episode earned me a dubious nickname with the crew.)

So to point out the painfully obvious; communication is key to everything you do while in another country. (Believe it or not there are still American tourists who tend to assume that everyone speaks English, or at least understands it if it is yelled at them long and loud enough.) Before you start your trip, learn some of the language. Knowing how to say hello, thank you and a few other basic phrases will earn you the respect of your hosts and probably open doors on your visit that would otherwise not be available to you. Besides, it's fun to be able to order boiled yak tail in the local language. You might also want to check out (as in, buy) one of the editions (World, Central Europe or Northern Europe) of the book *New Theatre Words* published by the Secretariat General of OISTAT and sold by USITT. It's got a ton of extremely helpful stage terms in a bunch of different languages.

Once you get to your destination, you will probably find that at least someone speaks some English. You should make friends with that someone. You will also find pointing, body language, facial expressions and the occasional grunt to be useful. I know this sounds like lunch break in the scene shop, but hey, whatever works. If there's no one around who speaks English and you really really need someone to interpret, head for the schools. Most major cities have an American school that caters to expatriates and members of the diplomatic corp. You should be able to hire someone to translate for you. I've had great success with this in Asian countries. Or go to the local college or university. If there's a theatre department, great; you can get someone there. Even if there's no theatre department you can usually find someone who is willing work as a translator.

Communication difficulties are not always verbal. I highly recommend that you check the equipment your crew is using.

Especially their measuring tools. Are their tape measures metric, but your blueprints in feet-and-inches? Could be their tape measures are in feet-and-inches, but are calibrated so that ten inches equals a foot. This might just present a problem, which of course I learned the hard way. It was after we had finished installing the T-bar guides for a counterweight system that I discovered this little quirk. We had to go back and pick up the entire wall (about 2,500 pounds) and move it nine inches downstage. Not fun.

Materials are different around the world and things that you may be accustomed to are not necessarily available in a foreign country. Be careful what you ask for! Most local crews really want to help and do the job right, so when you need some lumber, check out the type and sizes that are readily available. You could drive your crew crazy asking for a mess of 1 x 3 pine when all that is around is ¾" mahogany. And you might end up waiting for a few weeks.

Getting equipment in and out of the country can be particularly trying. It may seem that customs rules change on a minute-by-minute basis. (In some places, that may very well be true.) Patience and an even temperament will go a long way to help you through the process. It also helps to remember that the laws are different in many places and you might find it necessary to do something you would never dream of doing in the States just to get your gear off the dock and into the theatre. Check with as many local authorities as you can before you do anything, however. Be aware that there are things we do here that would be illegal in some other places. When in Rome...

Local customs can be different and confusing. Check them out before you go. In Arabic countries, for example, you never point at anyone. It's considered very impolite. When you're in Canada it is considered bad form to call people from the States "Americans." If you'll check a map you'll discover that Canada is in North America and, it follows, that Canadians get to be Americans too! And while belching may be considered polite in some countries, France is not one of them.

For me one of the most fun aspects of travel is the food. I love food. Being able to try new things in another country is heaven as far as I'm concerned. But, over the years, I've learned a few lessons. Most important: eat where the locals eat. Don't go running off to McDonald's as soon as you get a meal break. You can get Mickey D's at home, for crying out loud. How many places in the States serve live snake? If you visit one of the night markets in Asia, not only can you get snake, but also eel, spider, lizard and some other stuff that you may not want to identify. And not all of it tastes like chicken. But stay away from the food stalls for the first few days. Give your stomach a chance to get acclimated. Ask the local crew for some nearby restaurant recommendations. I'd be willing to bet they'd be happy to take you and introduce you to some of the local cuisine. Once you've sampled the restaurant fare, you might be ready for the more adventuresome stuff in the night markets and food stands.

The biggest joy I get in working overseas is the people that I meet and friends I have made. I once mentioned to a Chinese friend that I was getting married and he showed up at the wedding! Another time I was having breakfast in Finland with a Swede who was attending a seminar I was conducting. We were swapping stories about kids and I mentioned how my daughter's birthday was coming up. That evening I found a present for her in my room. He had left it just before he checked out of the hotel. I never did get a chance to thank him. And it was just a bit confusing one night when I was sitting in a hotel bar in Hong Kong listening to a Filipino band play country and western music. And doing a great job too!

So, as Kurt Vonnegut once wrote, "Unexpected invitations to travel are dancing lessons from heaven." Go, work and enjoy. And stay out of trouble.

Working Smart

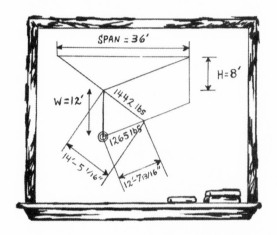

During a meeting I overheard someone say, several times, "That's the way we've always done it." Now, in the context of that discussion, the comments were appropriate. But I've heard the "this is the way we've always done it" argument before and it's rarely the right response. What I'd like to know is how do we really come to identify and solve a problem in this business?

Research and development (R & D) in the entertainment business has a rich and colorful history. Folklore would have us believe that the only true method for conducting R & D requires the aid of a cocktail napkin, the back of an envelope or a matchbook cover. I have also used the back of my hand to illustrate a stage effect. Whatever the method and medium, it boils down to one basic fact: In our little industry, at least in the rigging and scenic sectors, R & D has been more serendipitous than scientific.

We're a small industry and theatre folk are a transient lot. We tend to skip from one job to another the way other folks switch vacation spots. And because of that gypsy-like behavior, the solution for a problem at one place can easily travel from theatre to theatre and TV studio to theme park in short order. Before you know it the solution found at the break table becomes a "common practice." From common practice it's a short and inevitable walk to "industry standard." ("Common practice" and "industry standard" are, among other things, terms that can be used in court if there are no clear official guidelines or standards to point to.)

True R & D – the kind that follows all those pesky scientific guidelines – is time consuming and expensive. It is much easier and cheaper to sit down at lunch, draw up the problem on a napkin and then rummage around in the memory vaults of your crewmates for an appropriate solution. Invariably, someone comes up with a gizmo or piece of hardware that he has seen used by his sister's brother-in-law (the underwater fence repair technician for a salmon farm in Nova Scotia). The device is held aloft and those magic words are uttered, "Hey, think this'll work?"

At the risk of sounding like an old pharte, I'm more skeptical about this R & D procedure now than I was twenty years ago. Mainly, it's because I've come to realize that the solution found at the coffee break table may have worked well on that particular day for that particular problem at that particular theatre, but it is not necessarily appropriate for the rest of us. But now we have, as an industry standard, something that some TD thought up who knows where or when.

Wire rope clips (what many people call Crosby clips), for instance, are illegal for overhead lifting in many other countries. If you want to terminate wire rope in the theatre you have to use something that does not damage the wire rope. I've seen stage technicians in Finland use fasteners that do not damage the wire rope when installed nor do they require a special tool to tighten. Back here in the States most folks use wire rope clips out of habit. Years ago some TD somewhere decided clips were a good idea. Yes, there were other methods available, even in those prehistoric times.

Fist grips, wedge sockets and the like were, and still are, a much more efficient way to terminate wire rope. But they cost a lot more and that, my friends, is why we don't use them.

But here's some good news. I've discovered that many of today's rigging equipment manufacturers in the States do indeed test their products. They test them in-house and they use independent labs. Not only do they test finished products, like winches and loft blocks and arbors, but they also test components. This is a very cool thing and it's one of the reasons why you almost never hear of a failure in new rigging gear.

There's still a lot of equipment being installed in theatres that's the result of impromptu R & D. There are many homemade cable winches that are just plain dangerous. Some use belt drives and others use shaft couplings that aren't designed for suspended loads, let alone shock loads. And very few of them have any type of protective housing to keep sleeves, apron strings or fingers out of sprockets and chain drives.

I'm the last person to want to stifle the creativity of our technical people, but I also don't want to see people get hurt. Before putting that homemade device into practice, take a long hard look at the ramifications should it fail. Will the failure cause serious damage to your building? Could someone get hurt? If the answer is yes to either of these questions you should stop and get the device professionally tested before you start using it. There is probably a testing lab not too far away. The cost of a test (one pull) is determined by the complexity of the equipment that you want to test, but it usually starts around 100 dollars a pull. And lab engineers need some entertainment, just like the rest of us. They spend their days testing concrete core samples and bending I-beams. They love it when someone walks in with a batten clamp attached to some aircraft cable with a shackle. And they really light up when confronted with a piece of rope and a counterweight arbor.

I realize that some may think that what I'm suggesting isn't terribly practical. The reason many people think our technical design work is done in a bar on the back of a cocktail napkin is because, for better or for worse, a lot of it is. Unforeseen problems crop up at tech rehearsals all the time. And tech rehearsals don't usually end till late in the day, at best. The director needs (wants) a solution by morning. So you sit at the bar, wolf down some dinner and try to fix the problem. One of the complications these days is that the gear is a lot bigger, more intricate and moves faster than twenty years ago. Present day motorized winches commonly run at 200 to 400 feet per minute. Think about the damage a 2,000 pound deck piece would cause if it broke away from its wagon or track and was sent careening around a stage at that speed. It may be that we, as a group, have to learn how to say "no," or "give me more time," a little more often.

By the way, that meeting I referred to earlier was the Rigging Working Group; one of the many groups operating under the ESTA Technical Standards Committee (TSC). The TSC and the various working groups are committed to protecting the health and well being of all of us in the entertainment business by working on standards through the American National Standards Institute (ANSI). These standards help identify the proper way to manufacture, install and operate a wide range of equipment that we use on a daily basis.

If you'd like to know more about the TSC and any of the working groups, I invite you to stop by at www.esta.org.

Lessons Learned

His swagger as he walked down the aisle caught my eye. He had the kind of stride that said he owned the place. As he drew closer my heart sank and I knew my luck had run out. I was seated in 62G and there, printed on the boarding pass that he clutched tightly in both hands, was his seat number – 62F. This was a flight from Johannesburg to Atlanta by way of Cape Town and Isle de Sol. His name was Alamander and he was three years old. I realized that I was once again paying the penalty for not learning a lesson.

It's not like I've never made a mistake in my life. I stopped counting them a long time ago. But sometimes it takes a three-year-old to drive home the idea that you've got to learn from those mistakes. The error was that I had allowed a client to make my plane reservations for me. And this wasn't the first time. Did you know that it's possible to fly to Ecuador from New York City via Chicago *and* Miami? Or how about going to San Francisco from Philly via Dallas *and* Denver? In each case my client had booked the flights without consulting me. In the current case I should have been on the non-stop flight the day before, but no – I hadn't learned my lesson. So here I was facing a twenty-hour trip with Alamander, his slightly older sister and their grandmother as seat mates. Did I mention the kids only spoke Afrikaans? Yes, it was a very long night.

There had recently been a high-profile accident in Pretoria. An outdoor roof rig had collapsed during an awards ceremony. It happened in early August 2003. The president of South Africa was onstage. Fortunately he didn't get hurt, but Ms. Suraya Scott, who was there to receive an award, did. She was permanently paralyzed. Until I got to Durban I had seen only still photos of the event. In Durban I saw the video and it scared the hell out of me. I have seen some bad rigging in my day, but to watch an entire structure collapse in less than five seconds is right there at the top of my list of things I don't ever want to see again. Like most accidents, it was avoidable. And, like most accidents, it was stupid. But that's not why I brought it up.

It was my perception of what happened in the days and weeks after the collapse that I found interesting. There was the usual government investigation, of course. The report came out a day or two before I arrived in Johannesburg. By the time I got to Cape Town, many people, in fact most of the folks attending my sessions had read it. They weren't all that interested in whose fault it was. What they were was worried that it could happen again and that they didn't have enough experience to prevent it. They came to the sessions prepared to ask questions on how to avoid that kind of problem (and many others) in the future. And they wanted answers.

That same summer I saw the following news items:

- A set piece fell in Philadelphia and nearly smacked a Supreme Court justice.

- An entire truss rig came down in Atlantic City narrowly missing a number of stagehands.

- The wind blew over a roof rig in Nebraska.

There were others that just didn't make the papers.

A truss snapped during the load-in of a nationally known rock band on tour. They simply replaced the truss. No blood, no foul, I guess.

A guy called me up and ordered three (count 'em, 3) counterweight arbors to replace ones broken in recent runaway type accidents. What was he doing over there, a demolition derby?

And I got a call from a friend who had dropped off the radar for a while. Seems he had put in a 120 hour work week and then had a bit of a breakdown. No? Really? And after only 120 hours? Go figure.

So now I have a question. How many of you know whether a report has or has not been made public regarding any of the major accidents over the past five years or so? I know you've seen the pictures because they're on the Internet within five minutes of the time of the accident. But has a report of any kind been issued? And if there is a report, how many of you have read it? How many of you know what happened on that stage, and why?

This, my friends, is where I think we may have a bit of a problem. We tend to move on too easily. No one died, so very few people take the time to find out what really happened. We get caught up in our own projects and lose track of the bigger picture. But burying our collective heads in the sand won't make these accidents go away and it won't solve the problems that caused them.

So how do we learn from past mistakes, not only our own, but also the ones other people make? Learning takes communication. It takes a dialog between interested parties. Talk to your peers. Talk with those you know and respect in the industry. Talk about what may have caused the accident and what you might have done if you were in a similar situation. Find out if a report has been issued and then read it. Don't stop asking questions until you get some answers.

These accidents happened because people weren't paying attention. Someone who was paying attention would have known to bolt the rig down or put ballast on the base plates. If someone had simply taken the time to assess the situation without worrying about what was supposed to happen in an hour or two, maybe, just maybe, Ms. Scott would be walking today and former Justice O'Connor wouldn't be scratching Philadelphia off her vacation list.

I mentioned some of the causes of accidents way back in Chapter 1, but I think it would be good to have another look. This is critical stuff, after all. For whatever reasons, it's always a constant battle to stay within the production budget. Everyone is looking for shortcuts to save some money. Now I've got a business to run just like the other guys, and I'm all for saving a few bucks, but not at the expense of safety.

In my experience one of the first things to get cut are the special effects rehearsals. Someone sitting in an office drinking his latte will decide it's okay to rehearse the flight sequence while the regular rehearsal is going on. It's not okay. The special effects folks need their own rehearsal to work out the timing and the logistics with the performers. That's one of the reasons they call them "special" effects.

And what's with this working a zillion hours a week? Maybe the crew was being rushed or just plain tired. Maybe they had three other gigs to do that day and they weren't focusing on the details of any of them. Focus on the project at hand. If you can't focus because you're too tired or the boss has you running in circles, stop working. Take a break. Do something that will allow you to go back to the task at hand with a clearer head.

What would happen if you were so damn tired during the strike that you forgot to use your fall arrest harness for that "one last climb" of the night and you took a header off the truss. Is it worth it? Of course not. There have been many studies conducted on the effects of working for too many hours and on sleep deprivation. You have got to take a stand at some point and say "No – enough is enough." Yes, you may lose some pay over it and you might even lose your job. But that's a lot better than ending up in a hospital. Or worse.

Along with the exhaustion syndrome there's also the communication thing. That ability humans have to convey feelings, thoughts, needs and desires to one another. When communication breaks down, trouble is around the corner. The Philly incident is a prime example. The report released to the public regarding the National Constitution Center accident noted that there were a "multitude of missteps" that led up to the accident and that most of those missteps revolved around poor or non-existent communications between the staff, crew and event management. It appears that everyone had been working around the clock and there wasn't enough time to get everything done. Special effects were put into the show at the last minute, removed and then reinstated. Individual decisions were made without a clear understanding of the whole picture. There was no time for rehearsals. People did not or could not talk to each other. The result was that some people got hurt.

It's great that we're so much more safety conscious than we were five or ten years ago. Fall arrest is no longer something to be scorned. I conduct more seminars each year than the previous year. And, thanks to people like Harry Donovan and Rocky Paulson, more people know how to figure bridle leg lengths and loads than ever before. But, given the type of accidents we saw in just one summer, it seems to me that maybe we've somehow missed the fundamentals. Have we, in our rush to be as aware as possible of the big stuff, hurdled over the basics? Have we missed out on Backstage 101? Are we, as a group, becoming too cavalier with the knowledge that we think we posses? Sure, people were dead tired when that frame was put up and the ribbons rigged, but why wasn't there one person, just one, who stopped and said "Yo. Hold up a sec. Youse guys gonna anchor this thing down or what? Cause if you don't it's gonna fall over."

When accident reports are released, you should take the time to read them. I know it's sounds pretty boring but it's a great way to learn from mistakes – other peoples' mistakes. The official government report on the Pretoria, South Africa accident is called the "Report on the Collapse of the Marquee at the Union Buildings on the 9th August 2003" and is available at www.gpg.gov. za/docs/reports/2003/marquee.html.

So if I, stubborn old coot *extraordinaire*, can finally learn a lesson (with the assistance of my traveling companion from South Africa), then there's got to be hope for the rest of you. From now on I'll book my own flights and we'll all try to keep things from falling down. And I want you to work smart and safe.

Certification

In the fall of 2005 the Entertainment Technician Certification Program (ETCP) unveiled its theatre and arena rigging certification exams. These exams were followed one year later by the electrical certification exam. Now, these exams didn't just appear out of thin air. They were the result of a considerable amount of hard work by a number of industry professionals.

Time out for a quick history lesson. Although the concept of certification had been discussed for many years, it wasn't until 2002 that it really began to take on a form. Committees were formed within ESTA to investigate just what a certification program should look like and who should organize it. Out of these discussions the ETCP was formed. The ETCP then hired a professional certification company to help develop and administer the program and professionals from within the entertainment industry were brought on to help write the tests. It was, by all accounts, a Herculean effort by a number of very dedicated people, but the end result was a program that worked very well and continues to do so.

So why did we need this program in the first place? And why do we need it now?

Take a quick look around. The shows are getting larger and more complex. When Bette Midler went out on tour with a 120,000 pound rig, many people thought we had reached an unbeatable milestone. The very next year Paul McCartney was out with 150,000 pounds. Who knows what next year will bring.

One only has to wander backstage at a Cirque du Soleil production to get a glimpse of how complex a show can become. But with the size and complexity come a higher degree of responsibility. You can't run shows the way you did ten years ago. The control systems alone require a level of expertise previously unheard of in our business, not to mention that all this gear needs someone to maintain it properly. But where do you find these people? How do you measure the skill level of the person standing in front of your desk, interviewing for a job, without relying solely on a résumé?

Let's be honest. As an industry, we've got a bunch of people working around the country who profess to know what they are doing. Many do, but some, unfortunately, do not. Wouldn't it be nice to be able to tell one from the other? And wouldn't it be great if we, as professional riggers and electricians, had a method to show the world what our skill level is in our chosen field? This is where the ETCP comes in.

The ETCP has designed the certification exams to be tools to measure the skill level of professional riggers and electricians in North America. The rigging certification exam is divided into two categories, one for theatrical riggers and one for arena riggers. These exams target the top third of the professionals in each of these two disciplines. It would not be much of an exam if it tried to cover everyone in the field, eh? The exams consist of 150 multiple-choice questions. (As a reward for reading, i.e. buying, this book, here are the answers to the tests. A, B, C, D. I just can't remember their order.)

The ETCP uses a point system to screen candidates who wish to sit for the test. As I noted earlier, the primary method for accumulating points is through work. The expectation is that people with at least three years of rigging experience will qualify to take the test. We are looking for the top third of the discipline's population, after all. The point system helps to screen out the overzealous student or inexperienced technician. The ETCP does not want people spending their hard earned money on a test that they're not ready to take. The folks at the ETCP have put together an informative website that should answer most of your questions, www.etcp.esta.org. On the site you will find not only a current list of certified technicians but also the ETCP Recognized employers, labor providers and trainers. ETCP Candidate Handbooks are also available as PDF downloads for riggers and electricians.

Before you ask yourself if you need to be certified, take a look at the type of work you do. Are you consistently the lead rigger or electrician on a tour? Do you take a show concept and design the systems to make the show work? Do you spend a lot of your time in the high steel making hoist points and bridle legs? Do you do power tie-ins on a regular basis? Then yes, you probably should take the test. You should probably take the test if you're the head flyman or electrician on a theatrical tour. Same is true if you're the head rigger or electrician at the big road house in town. Ditto if you are responsible for overseeing permanent installations on a regular basis.

As more venues and organizations begin to require that their lead technicians become certified, and as more specifications are written with the requirement that the lead installer be certified, it will follow that more and more technicians will become certified. As of this writing there are over 325 certified technicians in North America and more come on board every month. Don't look now but it appears that certification programs are here to stay.

Around the World in Eighty Meals

While scanning the news on the internet one day I came upon a startling statistic. There are about 26,000 vehicle crashes yearly in the US caused by animals. Half of the accidents involve cars running off the road to avoid the animal. In the other half, the vehicles make contact. Most accidents involve deer, although bears, raccoons and squirrels are well represented. So naturally, I started thinking about lunch.

There's a restaurant in Johannesburg called Carnivore. Its menu is pretty much what you'd expect. Meat, meat and more meat. And beer. The placed is set up with long tables that accommodate about twenty-five people at a time. You sit and drink beer. The servers bring out spits of meat and offer you a slice or two. But this isn't your run of the mill cow joint. This is the exotic stuff. There's antelope, eland, crocodile, ostrich and wart hog (Pumba on a stick) to name just a few. It's good fun. You get to compare notes with your tablemates – "Hey, try the giraffe. It tastes just like chicken." – and drink lots of beer. The South Africans do know their way around beer. The local stuff is really good. The only sour note in the evening came when I asked the server if the wildebeest he was serving was road kill. He didn't answer the question but his eyes got wide and he walked off shaking his head. Didn't slow me down any though.

It always seems that when I have several trips stacked one after another, a common thread, a theme, if you will, tends to weave the various places together. You know how it can go. When you're on a tour there's a dimmer rack that gives you trouble show after show, or maybe the concierges at all the Holiday Inns are named Mike. One summer my theme turned out to be food. And drink. Johannesburg had the meat. Capetown had the wine.

This was my third trip to South Africa and so I knew some people there. One night after a session we ended up at this guy's house for pizza and wine. As you may know, South Africa has been producing some very nice wines lately. I've found the reds to be particularly good. Well, at dinner our host brought out a bottle of red that was especially tasty. Nice full body and not too fruity. Just the way I like it. The problem was the bottles didn't have labels. We had no idea where the stuff came from or where we could get more. Turns out he had about a case or so of the stuff. I spent the rest of the night trying to figure out how I could steal a bottle or two, but he, not being stupid, kept them hidden in a cabinet. Guess I'll just have to go back and find my own.

And then there was Finland. A trip to Finland provided more than just a taste of the local fare. I got local culture too. Finnish sauna. One night after a training session a group of us (two Americans, a Dane, a Greek and two Finns) drove up to a country cabin for a sauna. You should understand that when a Fin talks about going out to the county, he means it. We'd been on the road for about two hours and we still weren't there. The road went from paved to unpaved to simply ruts in a field. I was beginning to think I was hearing banjo music, ya know? But then we came to this cabin on a lake. You know those post cards you get of the great scenery? Well, they were all shot at this lake. It was pretty amazing. Part of the ritual of sauna is to dive into the lake every fifteen minutes or so. What they don't tell you is that the damn lake water is only fifty degrees Fahrenheit. You spend fifteen minutes roasting in the sauna and then you dive into the lake. Yeah. That was fun. My dips in the water averaged 2.4 seconds. And what did we do in between all of this roasting and freezing? We drank beer. Lots of beer. I'm really hoping there weren't any cameras around.

Helsinki provided the food and drink part of the trip. The food was all about reindeer. Reindeer meat, to be more exact. It was tender, juicy and full of flavor. And it's low in fat, too. Who'd a thunk Dasher and Prancer could taste so good, and be healthy too? Just don't tell my kids. And what better way to wash down a side of Blitzen than with a tall glass of pine tar? Yup. That's right. Pine tar. From the land of the midnight sun and long dark winters comes a liqueur made from pine tar. The bottles I saw were labeled "Tervasnapsi," but I may have the spelling wrong. After a few glasses of the stuff things started getting a little fuzzy. This is a great beverage to have around if your friends like to raid your liquor cabinet. It's, as they say, an acquired taste and few people are interested in acquiring one. I did acquire a taste for it but forgot to bring some home. Guess I'll have to go back.

So. Getting hungry yet? Well, you better be. (Here comes one of the strangest and most forced segues in this book.) I travel overseas to teach rigging classes and to talk to other people who teach rigging classes. And these folks are very hungry. Hungry for information. They want to learn everything they can about this business. They want to be better at their jobs. They've seen the photos of the accidents and they don't want to make those mistakes. Or any mistakes, for that matter. They come to the sessions prepared to learn. They ask questions all day long and stay late to ask more. They are, for the most part, young, eager and willing to travel. And they firmly believe that better training is their key to success. You know what? They're right. So don't be surprised when some South African kid shows up on the job one day and makes up bridles better and faster than anyone else on site – and ends up with the road gig. You've been warned.

-9-
Reflections

Peter Feller, Sr.

Many of us have someone in our past who affected us in a big way. Someone who touched our soul and helped us become more than we ever thought we could be. Mentor is the word most commonly used to describe that person but somehow, in my case, mentor doesn't seem right. The word just isn't big enough.

Peter L. Feller, Sr., a two-time Tony Award-winning builder of sets for hundreds of Broadway shows, died on March 13, 1998 at the Holmes Regional Hospital in Melbourne, Florida. He was seventy-eight.

There are many people in our industry who have never heard the name Peter Feller. But their lives and careers were touched by him and his work. I was very fortunate to meet Peter early in my career. It was 1973 at the Zellerbach Theatre in Philadelphia. He was bringing tryouts there for the New York Shakespeare Festival and the Phoenix Company.

His father was a master set builder in the 1930s and Peter followed in his footsteps. His career began with *This is the Army* with Irving Berlin. He was the TD, responsible for building the set and moving it around Europe during World War II. For the next fifty-plus years Peter ran scenery studios. First at Yankee Stadium, then in the Bronx and finally on Stewart Airbase in Newburgh, New York. To list the names of the shows he was responsible for would overflow this space. *A Chorus Line, Cats, Cabaret, Sweeney Todd...* You get the idea. Add to that list the names of the designers and producers he worked with and you have a veritable Who's Who of the theatre business.

Peter was the consummate craftsman. His attention to detail was legendary. It had to look right, absolutely right, or it wasn't good enough. He was someone who cared and a person you could depend on. When I moved to New York and was trying to get onto Broadway, I went to see him about a job. He stopped what he was doing to listen to my story and put me to work right then and there. The fact that he was onstage of the Schubert Theater loading in *A Chorus Line* and had about thirty guys standing around didn't matter. He always listened.

Peter loved this business and the people in it. He was a mentor, friend and critic. If you asked his opinion you had to be prepared for a direct answer because that's what you'd get. When he spoke, you listened. When he yelled, you listened closer. He may have been gruff on the outside, but he really was the ultimate teddy bear. And above all else, he was honest and fair.

I'm proud to have had the opportunity to work with Peter Feller. He may not have been the reason I got into theatre, but he was one of the reasons I stayed.

London

In 2006 I went to London for the Theatre Engineering and Architecture (TEA) Conference and the Association of British Theatre Technicians (ABTT) Theatre Show. I was to be speaking at both events and my goal was to not make a complete fool of myself. The weather in London in early June is supposed to be very nice – a little cool and low humidity. Not this year. When I got off the plane at Heathrow I thought maybe I'd landed in the wrong place. It was ninety-five degrees Fahrenheit outside. The hotel was not air-conditioned, of course, but they did pass out pedestal fans for each of the rooms. At least it kept the air moving.

The TEA Conference was held on Great George Street, just up the road from Big Ben and around the corner from St. James Park. It's hard to imagine a better place to hold an event. The conference rooms are beautiful and the great hall is amazing – murals on the ceiling and paneling on the walls. It was air-conditioned too. Well over 400 professionals joined in over thirty-five sessions dedicated to discussing the issues and challenges we all face in designing new and renovated performance spaces. More than ninety speakers presented their views on topics ranging from future trends in automation to the design of the orchestra pit and stage engineering standards.

To me, the conference represented something akin to a miracle. Gathered here were many of the top architects, consultants, engineers and equipment manufacturers from all over Europe, and some from the States, and they actually listened to each other. There was a genuine interest in other points of view. There were lively debates over things like the bid process (it's called tendering in the UK), and what's really happening in and to the fly tower. Egos, for the most part, were left at the door. I have to believe that even if only ten percent of what was discussed in the forums makes its way out into the world, this conference will have served its purpose admirably.

Richard Brett is the gentleman who put this together, along with a very capable staff led by Catherine Cooper. Richard is to be commended for not only bringing together such an august body of experts but also for giving the speakers the latitude to speak their minds. These discussions were not for the faint of heart. The Q & A was intense and to the point. People came prepared to discuss problems and they wanted, and got, answers. Woe to the speaker who went soft or tried to dodge a question.

Catherine and her team held us all together. Lunches were delicious and on time. The air-conditioner was wheedled, cajoled and downright begged to keep up and, somehow, it did. And she saved my butt when she printed a copy of my ABTT speech after I had lost the original.

Given the amount of information that was careening around the rooms at any given time, it's hard to believe that anyone could walk away from this conference without having something to think about. The next TEA is being planned for three or four years from now and I would urge anyone who has a vested interest in performance spaces to attend. I also think that there should be a conference like the TEA held here in the States, but that's a subject for another time.

Which now brings me to the Association of British Theatre Technicians. I've been coming to their Theatre Show for a number of years and it never ceases to impress me. The show takes place in the Horticultural Halls just off Vincent Square. The first year I attended it occupied just one small floor in one building. The stands (booths to us back on this side of the pond) were small and crammed together like salmon on a fish farm.

Since then the show has grown into three floors in two buildings. The halls are still small and the stands are shoved in to every available space. There's not much room to move around and sometimes it's hard to tell where one stand stops and the next one starts. It may not sound that great to those of you used to the more spacious shows in the States, but it works very well. There is an energy level like no other show I've ever attended. The buzz in the room is genuine; it's not the sound system. The place feels like a *souk* in Istanbul where all the vendors know each other and look out for each other. This show is about the British theatre family. This year (2006) about 2,400 "family members" visited. Not bad for an organization with around 1,700 members, eh?

I would be remiss if I did not mention the lunch spot out back on Horse Ferry Road that Siobhan from Rope Assemblies Ltd. turned me on to during my first visit. It's still there and it's still serving the best quick lunch I've had in London. The turkey, bacon and avocado sandwich on brown bread is my favorite. The place is called Joe's or Eat at Joe's or something like that and it's just a block off Vincent Square. It has a blue awning and, especially around noon, a line out the door.

Meanwhile, back at the show, Roger Fox – who has been the show director since the beginning – is always walking around checking on the stands and making sure everything goes smoothly. This is definitely his baby and he thoroughly enjoys showing her off. The buzz is in the air. It's crowded and the stands are full of people checking out the gear. Roger is obviously very pleased.

There are some panel discussions and some presentations, but it's really the trade show that draws the people. It's about the gear and catching up with old friends. I make no bones about my fondness for this group. I came over here several years ago with my then 14-year-old daughter, Jordan. As I walked in from the street on the first day, I was greeted by four of five people, all of them British. Jordan looked up at me in surprise and with a newfound respect (lost, I'm afraid, when she hit sixteen) because I had friends in London. Like I said earlier – family.

I believe Richard Pilbrow, at the closing plenary meeting of the TEA, said it best. This industry is all about people. It's live theatre. It's about being in that one very special moment when a performer makes you gasp and the hair on the back of your neck stands up. We should never lose sight of that and, if the TEA and the ABTT are any indication, I don't think we will. So join me next June as I once again visit with my friends and compatriots in London. I'll be the guy on the left with the beer in one hand and waving a fan with the other.

Voting

A citizen of America will cross the ocean to fight for democracy, but won't cross the street to vote in a national election. – Bill Vaughan

I grew up in the '50s and '60s in blue-collar suburbia, row homes as far as the eye could see. The neighborhood was chock full of kids and, when we weren't in school, we ran from dawn till dusk. Baseball, hide and seek, basketball, football; you name it we did it. I had a blast.

My father wasn't an immigrant. His family had come over from Russia several generations earlier. My mother's parents had recently emigrated from Genoa, Italy. Neither was overtly patriotic. My father loved taking me to parades but mainly because he liked to listen to the bands. Mom was a little more enthusiastic. She would help us decorate our bikes every Fourth of July. Looking back I can see how, in the little things they did – the flags going up on the holidays, the membership at the VFW and volunteering with the little league – they both recognized, enjoyed and valued their good fortune at living in the USA.

Dad was a postman and so I had a little more contact with the government than most of the other kids I knew. But I really didn't much care what was going on in the outside world as long as my world continued to be fun. If I had paid attention to the grown ups I would have noticed that the adults in my world didn't always share my enthusiasm for the times. I vaguely remember the quiet discussions my parents sometimes had at dinner. Occasionally Dad would sit on the front stoop and talk with our next-door neighbor, Jack. They mostly talked sports and neighbors and stuff, but sometimes the talk turned to politics. Apparently there was a lot going on.

What did I know about the cold war and Cuba and segregation? Being eight, nothing had much of an impact on me unless it involved getting dirty. But then, when I was ten or so, my father took me to an election. Not a convention or anything – I simply got to go with him when he went to vote. I remember going to the polling station with him and seeing all the people standing around outside wearing buttons and handing out pieces of paper. I remember going inside the voting booth. And I remember the smell (it was, after all, in the grade school gym). But, for some reason, I can't remember what the voting machine looked like.

You know that old saying, "If you remember the '60s you weren't there"? Well I was there and I remember them. The Kennedy assassination left its mark, as it did with everyone. I was in the fifth grade in Sister Mary Margaret's class. Then came the Beatles and rock and roll, girls and drugs. (Not necessarily in that order.) Yeah, it was fun, and, at least for the first couple of years, high school was great. Then word started going around about Vietnam. And soldiers going over there to fight. And then the older brother of a friend was killed there. And, slowly, things began to change. The outside world started to intrude into my life to a degree that could not be ignored.

I did a lot of things during those years. Some of them a little more foolish than others and some a little less legal. I'm not ashamed or sorry for any of it. I was glad to be alive and happy to survive. I didn't register for everything in the '60s and '70s, but I did register to vote. And I voted in every election that came around.

I'm not exactly sure why voting was so important to me. My parents always voted so I knew a little about it. I guess some of their understated happiness for living in this country rubbed off on me. As I got older things became a little clearer. I suspect one of the reasons I voted was to hedge my bets. Somewhere along the line I think I realized that my outside activities might not be enough to affect the kind of social change I was looking for. Nor would those activities necessarily preserve the things I didn't want to see changed. I guess I felt that voting was yet another way of accomplishing my goals.

And, if I'm going to be truly honest with myself, I voted because I wanted the right to bitch and complain. I wanted to be able to whine about the folks who were running the country when they did so in a manner not to my liking. And I knew that if I didn't vote I forfeited the right to whine.

Those of you who have read this far know I love to travel. One of those reasons is that I love knowing, no matter where I am or what people think or say about Americans, I get to go home to the USA. I love knowing that, when the rhetoric is over and the dust from one crisis or another has settled, I still live in the USA.

It doesn't matter what your political persuasion is or what label you take on for yourself. Most of you who are reading this live in the USA. You get to do all kinds of really cool things that many, many other people in this world would kill (and sometimes die) for. You have more freedom than anyone else on the planet. And you know it.

Our industry is founded on the freedom guaranteed to us by the Constitution. We have always prided ourselves on having the ability to publish any book we want or make any movie we want or produce any kind of play we want. This not a Republican Party freedom or a Democratic Party freedom, or even an Independent Party freedom. It's an American freedom.

And the best way to protect that freedom is to participate in the process. This means voting. I'm not sure what other incentives are needed to convince you to cross that street and vote. Maybe it's showing the rest of the world that we really are the good guys. Or maybe it's simply that when you vote you get complaining rights for the following four years. Whatever the reason, I hope I see you at the polls the next time an election comes around.

Oh, and one more thing: when you go to the polling station, take your kids.

LDI

I'm here in Vegas attending the LDI 2004 conference. At the moment I'm sitting next to the fountain in front of the Venetian Hotel watching the world go by. For my money this is one of the best tickets in town. (It's certainly the least expensive.) It's Vegas, after all and all manner of folk come here. (The couple that just walked by in rumpled evening wear hasn't drawn any attention, not even a raised eyebrow, even though it's 8:30 in the morning.)

I should probably tell you that I'm not a big Vegas fan. I don't gamble and my taste in entertainment runs to the small, intimate theatre experience. I'm also not all that fond of trade shows. I go to them mainly because for years it's been drilled into my head that if I don't show my face, people will think I'm dead, in jail, or bankrupt. Given a choice, I'd be on my motorcycle somewhere out in the desert.

Those who don't go to these trade shows have the impression that we're all here to party. You know the image; guy in a suit, wearing a lampshade and towing a blonde. The truth is, after an eight-hour day of walking, talking and standing around, I'm wanting a nap, not a party. Judging by the conversations I have with other exhibitors, most everyone else is in the same boat. Let's face it, once you reach a certain age your priorities shift from debauchery to putting your feet up and calling home to talk to the kids.

Could someone please tell me why it's so damn important to have every follow spot in the show shining across the room at exactly eye level? Do people really buy lighting equipment based on its ability to blind audience members? And what's with the wiggle lights? I'm betting that there are now enough moving light manufacturers to individually illuminate every pole dancer in Vegas. But all that fancy technology doesn't seem to apply to the PA system. This is an entertainment technology show, yes? You would think that we could enjoy a sound system that doesn't garble the announcements beyond recognition. I swear that the A train in New York has a better sound system.

And what's with the models at these shows??? Do some of these vendors really think that the only way to get people to stop by their booth is to decorate it with young women wearing knee high boots and practically nothing else? What did the dancer in that eight-foot plastic bubble have to do with anything? When I see these girls I don't think, gee, I better buy that lighting fixture over there. What I usually think is, "Can I get you a hamburger? Or at least a pretzel? Eat something already."

And speaking of food, everybody, and I do mean everybody, complains about the about the quality and prices of the food offered at the kiosks in the exhibit hall. And it's not just at this show; it's every show I've ever been to. I have never had anyone come up to me and say, "Hey Bill, you should try the twelve dollar Caesar salad that's been sitting on the shelf over there all week. It's really good." So, if no one likes the food, why are we still eating it? Maybe if we tried a little civil disobedience we might improve things a bit. A sit-in around the hot dog stand just might work. If nothing else it would get us off our feet for a few minutes.

So maybe you're thinking to yourself, "quit your bitching and stop going to the shows already." Well, beside the negative publicity you get if you don't go, these shows do have their moments.

You do get to see some new products (or at least older products tweaked to look new). There is the usual cast of characters – the lighting and truss guys along with the rigging and sound folks. You can't walk twenty feet without running into another LED wall. And you really do get to talk about the people who didn't make it to the show and wonder if they're dead, bankrupt or in jail somewhere. Best of all, you get to see old friends.

This is the only career I've ever had, so I have no idea what other industries are like, but I gotta tell you, the camaraderie in our little industry is amazing. Where else do you get to sit down at dinner with friends, one of them being a competitor you just beat out for a project, and laugh yourself silly about work, the kids and that one damn vendor who's driving everyone crazy? And just in case you hadn't noticed lately, this industry is full of really great people who lead very interesting lives. It's a lot of fun to hang out every once in a while and listen to their jokes and travel stories. No disrespect to the accountants of the world, but I really doubt they can describe a trip to a shipyard in Venice the way I heard it over dinner one night.

And this business is full of people who care very deeply about the work and their chosen profession. These people come to the convention to talk about their passion and find ways to improve the industry. They come to share ideas for designing shows that help make going to concert or the theatre an even better experience. Others come to listen and to take that fire back home with them and spread it around a little bit. The ESTA and ETCP meetings are held at these shows and they are not boring at all. Take a room full of highly intelligent, articulate and passionate people who want to make the world a better place through entertainment, and you're in for a remarkably good time.

And one last note. Every time I leave Las Vegas there's always a gaggle of little old ladies waiting in the gate area for their flight home. They sit around knitting and chatting about their grandkids and their ailments. And, with a sense of awe in their voices that is almost palpable, they recount their experiences in one casino after another. Invariably, one of these sweet blue haired ladies, after going on and on about all the neat stuff in Vegas and the big hotels and the buffets, will turn to a friend and say, "I wonder where they get the money to pay for all this?" I wonder where indeed.

See you at the next show.